Daily 6-Trait Writing GRADE 1

Editorial Development: Roseann Erwin
Joy Evans
Leslie Sorg
Andrea Weiss
Copy Editing: Cathy Harber
Art Direction: Cheryl Puckett
Cover Design: Liliana Potigian
Illustrators: Ann Iosa
Mary Rojas
Design/Production: Carolina Caird

EMC 6021

Evan-Moor
EDUCATIONAL PUBLISHERS®
Helping Children Learn since 1979

Congratulations on your purchase of some of the finest teaching materials in the world.

Correlated
to State Standards

Photocopying the pages in this book is permitted for single-classroom use only. Making photocopies for additional classes or schools is prohibited.

MW01493387

Contents

Daily 6-Trait Writing contains 25 weeks of mini-lessons divided into five units. Each unit provides five weeks of scaffolded instruction focused on one of the following traits: **Ideas**, **Organization**, **Word Choice**, **Sentence Fluency**, and **Voice**. (See pages 6–9 for more information about each of these, as well as the sixth trait, **Conventions**.) You may wish to teach each entire unit in consecutive order, or pick and choose the lessons within the unit.

Each week of *Daily 6-Trait Writing* focuses on a specific skill within the primary trait, as well as one Convention skill. The weeks follow a consistent five-day format, making *Daily 6-Trait Writing* easy to use.

Teacher Overview Pages

Trait Skill

A specific writing skill for each trait is targeted.

Reduced Pages

Reduced student pages provide sample answers.

Convention Skill

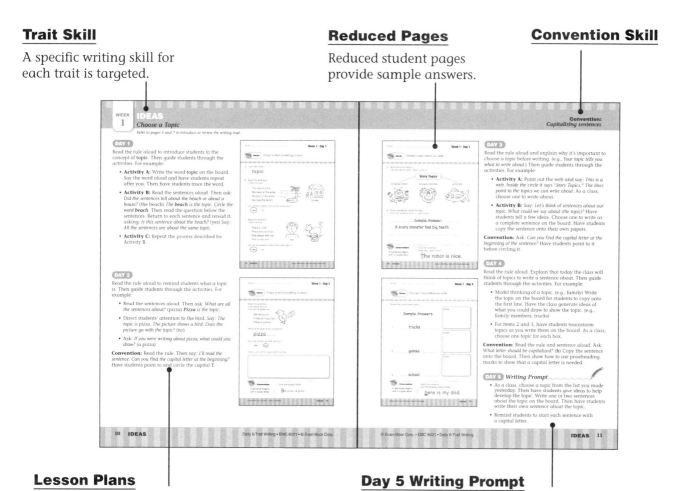

Lesson Plans

Use the lesson plans to teach the trait and Convention skills and guide students through the activities on Days 1–4. The plans are structured to enable you to differentiate and tailor lessons for your own class, but still provide the explanation and support you need. You may choose to have students complete the activities as a class, in small groups, or independently.

Day 5 Writing Prompt

Give your students the writing prompt to apply the trait and Convention skills in their own writing. Provide students with paper, or use the page provided for Day 5 in the student practice book. You may also wish to expand the writing prompt into a more fully developed assignment that takes students through the writing process.

Student Activity Pages

Trait and Rule (Skill Summary)

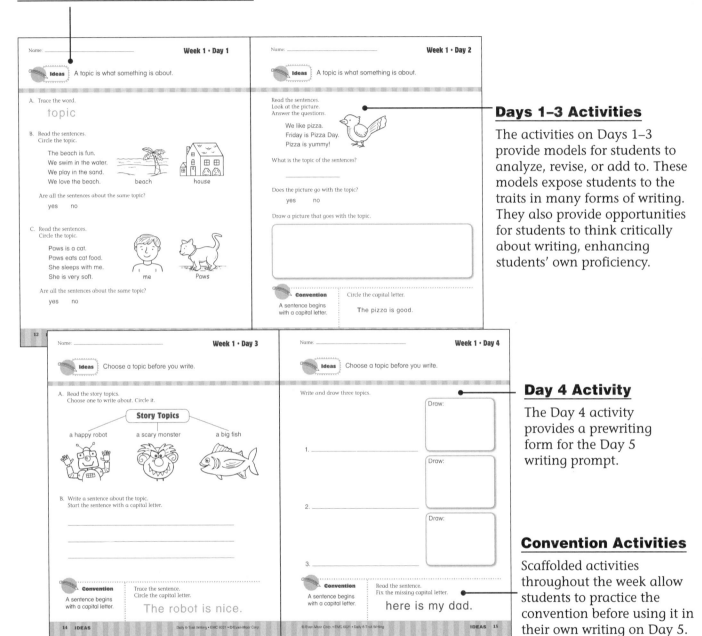

Days 1–3 Activities

The activities on Days 1–3 provide models for students to analyze, revise, or add to. These models expose students to the traits in many forms of writing. They also provide opportunities for students to think critically about writing, enhancing students' own proficiency.

Day 4 Activity

The Day 4 activity provides a prewriting form for the Day 5 writing prompt.

Convention Activities

Scaffolded activities throughout the week allow students to practice the convention before using it in their own writing on Day 5.

Ways to Use

There are many ways to integrate *Daily 6-Trait Writing* into your classroom:

- Teach the lessons trait by trait.
- Target and practice specific skills students need help with.
- Use the lessons to enhance writing workshops.
- Incorporate the lessons into your other writing programs.

Use these ideas to introduce or review the trait at the beginning of each unit.

Ideas

Explain to students that good writing starts with good ideas.

Say: *A good idea is clear, interesting, and original. It makes the reader say, "Wow!" or "I never would have thought of that!" Without good ideas, your writing would not have much of a point. Your reader would be bored!*

Organization

Explain to students that good writing is organized in a way that helps the reader understand the information and follow what the writer is saying.

Say: *The organization of your writing is what holds everything together. It puts your ideas in an order that makes sense, and it gives your writing a strong beginning, middle, and end. When your writing is not organized, your reader can grow confused and lose interest.*

Word Choice

Explain to students that good writers choose their words carefully in order to get their ideas across.

Say: *When you write, choose just the right words and use them correctly. Make them fun and interesting so they help your readers "see" what you are talking about. Try not to use the same words over and over again. If you don't choose your words carefully, your reader may not understand what you're trying to say.*

Sentence Fluency

Explain to students that good writers make their writing flow by using different kinds of sentences.

Say: *You want your writing to be easy to read and follow. It should flow so smoothly and sound so interesting that people want to read it aloud! When your sentences don't flow, your writing sounds choppy and flat. Your reader would not want to read it aloud.*

Voice

Explain to students that when they write, their personality, or who they are, should shine through.

Say: *You want your writing to sound like you, and no one else! When you write, you show who you are through words. No matter what type of writing you do, always make sure it sounds like you. Otherwise, your reader may not care about what you have to say. In fact, your reader may not even know who wrote it!*

Conventions

Explain to students that good writers follow all the rules, or conventions, of writing, so their readers can easily read and understand the writing.

Say: *Using correct grammar, spelling, and punctuation when you write is important. When you don't follow the rules, your reader can become lost or confused. He or she may not know where one idea starts and another begins.*

Using the Rubric

Use the rubric on pages 8 and 9 to evaluate and assess your students' skill acquisition.

- Each week, evaluate students' responses to the Day 5 writing prompt using the criteria that correspond to the skills taught that week.

- For review weeks, use all the trait criteria to assess students' understanding of that trait as a whole.

- Use the entire set of criteria to occasionally assess students' writing across the traits.

- In student- and parent-teacher conferences, use the rubric to accurately and clearly explain what a student does well in writing, as well as what he or she needs to improve.

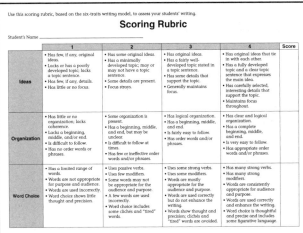

Use this scoring rubric, based on the six-traits writing model, to assess your students' writing.

Scoring Rubric

Student's Name _____

	1	2	3	4	Score
Ideas	• Has few, if any, original ideas. • Lacks or has a poorly developed topic; lacks a topic sentence. • Has few, if any, details. • Has little or no focus.	• Has some original ideas. • Has a minimally developed topic; may or may not have a topic sentence. • Some details are present. • Focus strays.	• Has original ideas. • Has a fairly well-developed topic stated in a topic sentence. • Has some details that support the topic. • Generally maintains focus.	• Has original ideas that tie in with each other. • Has a fully developed topic and a clear topic sentence that expresses the main idea. • Has carefully selected, interesting details that support the topic. • Maintains focus throughout.	
Organization	• Has little or no organization; lacks coherence. • Lacks a beginning, middle, and/or end. • Is difficult to follow. • Has no order words or phrases.	• Some organization is present. • Has a beginning, middle, and end, but may be unclear. • Is difficult to follow at times. • Has few or ineffective order words and/or phrases.	• Has logical organization. • Has a beginning, middle, and end. • Is fairly easy to follow. • Has order words and/or phrases.	• Has clear and logical organization. • Has a complete beginning, middle, and end. • Is very easy to follow. • Has appropriate order words and/or phrases.	
Word Choice	• Has a limited range of words. • Words are not appropriate for purpose and audience. • Words are used incorrectly. • Word choice shows little thought and precision.	• Uses passive verbs. • Uses few modifiers. • Some words may not be appropriate for the audience and purpose. • A few words are used incorrectly. • Word choice includes some clichés and "tired" words.	• Uses some strong verbs. • Uses some modifiers. • Words are mostly appropriate for the audience and purpose. • Words are used correctly but do not enhance the writing. • Words show thought and precision; clichés and "tired" words are avoided.	• Has many strong verbs. • Has many strong modifiers. • Words are consistently appropriate for audience and purpose. • Words are used correctly and enhance the writing. • Word choice is thoughtful and precise and includes some figurative language.	

Sentence Fluency	• Does not write complete sentences. • Has no variation in sentence structures and lengths. • Has no variation in sentence beginnings. • Has no cadence or flow in sentences.	• Has some incomplete sentences. • Has little variation in sentence structures and lengths. • Has little variation in sentence beginnings. • Sentences flow somewhat.	• Has 1 or 2 incomplete sentences. • Has some variation in sentence structures and lengths. • Has some variation in sentence beginnings. • Sentences flow fairly naturally.	• Has complete sentences. • Varied sentence structures and lengths contribute to the rhythm of the writing. • Varied sentence beginnings contribute to the flow of the writing. • Sentences flow naturally.
Voice	• Writing is neither expressive nor engaging. • Voice is not appropriate for the purpose, audience, topic, and/or genre. • Little evidence of an individual voice.	• Writing has some expression. • Voice is generally appropriate for the purpose, audience, topic, and/or genre. • Voice comes and goes.	• Writing is expressive and somewhat engaging. • Voice is appropriate for the purpose, audience, topic, and/or genre. • The voice is unique.	• Writing is very expressive and engaging. • Voice is consistently appropriate for the purpose, audience, topic, and/or genre. • The voice is unique, honest, and passionate.
Conventions	• Has multiple errors in grammar, punctuation, and mechanics. • Poor handwriting and/or presentation makes the writing hard to read. • Illustrations, if present, do not accurately portray the main idea.	• Has some errors in grammar, punctuation, and mechanics. • Handwriting and/or presentation is fairly clear. • Illustrations, if present, portray the main idea but do not enhance it.	• Has few errors in grammar, punctuation, and mechanics. • Handwriting and/or presentation is clear. • Illustrations, if present, accurately portray the main idea and enhance it somewhat.	• Has minimal errors in grammar, punctuation, and mechanics. • Handwriting and/or presentation of the piece is attractive and easy to read. • Illustrations, if present, enhance the main idea significantly.

TOTAL

IDEAS
Choose a Topic

Refer to pages 6 and 7 to introduce or review the writing trait.

DAY 1

Read the rule aloud to introduce students to the concept of **topic**. Then guide students through the activities. For example:

- **Activity A:** Write the word **topic** on the board. Say the word aloud and have students repeat after you. Then have students trace the word.

- **Activity B:** Read the sentences aloud. Then ask: *Did the sentences tell about the beach or about a house?* (the beach) *The **beach** is the topic. Circle the word **beach**.* Then read the question below the sentences. Return to each sentence and reread it, asking: *Is this sentence about the beach?* (yes) Say: *All the sentences are about the same topic.*

- **Activity C:** Repeat the process described for Activity B.

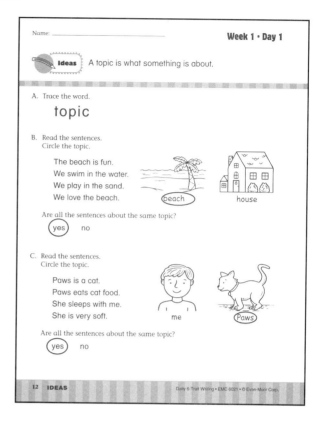

DAY 2

Read the rule aloud to remind students what a topic is. Then guide students through the activities. For example:

- Read the sentences aloud. Then ask: *What are all the sentences about?* (pizza) *Pizza is the topic.*

- Direct students' attention to the bird. Say: *The topic is pizza. The picture shows a bird. Does the picture go with the topic?* (no)

- Ask: *If you were writing about pizza, what could you draw?* (a pizza)

Convention: Read the rule. Then say: *I'll read the sentence. Can you find the capital letter at the beginning?* Have students point to and circle the capital **T**.

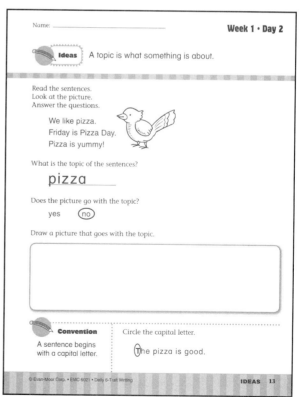

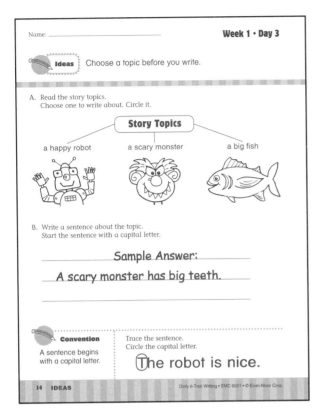

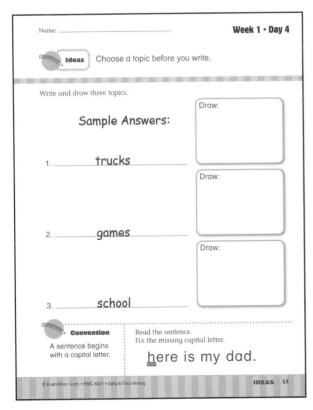

DAY 3

Read the rule aloud and explain why it's important to choose a topic before writing. (e.g., *Your topic tells you what to write about.*) Then guide students through the activities. For example:

- **Activity A:** Point out the web and say: *This is a web. Inside the circle it says "Story Topics." The lines point to the topics we can write about.* As a class, choose one to write about.

- **Activity B:** Say: *Let's think of sentences about our topic. What could we say about (the topic)?* Have students tell a few ideas. Choose one to write as a complete sentence on the board. Have students copy the sentence onto their own papers.

Convention: Ask: *Can you find the capital letter at the beginning of the sentence?* Have students point to it before circling it.

DAY 4

Read the rule aloud. Explain that today the class will think of topics to write a sentence about. Then guide students through the activities. For example:

- Model thinking of a topic. (e.g., family) Write the topic on the board for students to copy onto the first line. Have the class generate ideas of what you could draw to show the topic. (e.g., family members, trucks)

- For items 2 and 3, have students brainstorm topics as you write them on the board. As a class, choose one topic for each box.

Convention: Read the rule and sentence aloud. Ask: *What letter should be capitalized?* (**h**) Copy the sentence onto the board. Then show how to use proofreading marks to show that a capital letter is needed.

DAY 5 *Writing Prompt*

- As a class, choose a topic from the list you made yesterday. Then have students give ideas to help develop the topic. Write one or two sentences about the topic on the board. Then have students write their own sentence about the topic.

- Remind students to start each sentence with a capital letter.

Name: _____

 **Ideas**   A topic is what something is about.

A. Trace the word.

topic

B. Read the sentences.
Circle the topic.

The beach is fun.
We swim in the water.
We play in the sand.
We love the beach.

beach

house

Are all the sentences about the same topic?

yes   no

C. Read the sentences.
Circle the topic.

Paws is a cat.
Paws eats cat food.
She sleeps with me.
She is very soft.

me

Paws

Are all the sentences about the same topic?

yes   no

 **Ideas** A topic is what something is about.

Read the sentences.
Look at the picture.
Answer the questions.

We like pizza.
Friday is Pizza Day.
Pizza is yummy!

What is the topic of the sentences?

_____

Does the picture go with the topic?

yes   no

Draw a picture that goes with the topic.

 Convention

A sentence begins
with a capital letter.

Circle the capital letter.

The pizza is good.

 **Ideas** Choose a topic before you write.

A. Read the story topics.
Choose one to write about. Circle it.

Story Topics

a happy robot   a scary monster   a big fish

B. Write a sentence about the topic.
Start the sentence with a capital letter.

_____

_____

_____

Convention

A sentence begins
with a capital letter.

Trace the sentence.
Circle the capital letter.

The robot is nice.

 **Ideas** Choose a topic before you write.

Write and draw three topics.

1. _____

Draw:

2. _____

Draw:

3. _____

Draw:

 Convention

A sentence begins with a capital letter.

Read the sentence.
Fix the missing capital letter.

here is my dad.

DAY 1

Briefly review the meaning of **topic** from the previous week. (A topic is what something is about.) Then read the rule aloud and explain that one thing that makes writing good is a fun topic. Guide students through the activity. For example:

- Direct students to the first pair of pictures and ask: *Do you like milk? How about milk and cookies? Which is more fun to have?* Explain that the second picture shows a girl enjoying herself. It looks more fun. Have students write **milk and cookies** on the line.

- Direct students to the second pair of pictures and ask: *Have you ever splashed in a rain puddle? Isn't it fun?* Then point out the picture of the rain and say: *The picture of the rain is OK, but the picture of the boy splashing in a rain puddle looks more fun!* Have students write **splash** on the line.

DAY 2

Read the rule aloud and explain that today, students will learn more about choosing fun topics. Then guide students through the activities. For example:

- Read aloud the sentence pairs for the first picture. Then say: *The first pair of sentences is just about going to the park. The second pair of sentences tells one exciting thing that happened at the park.* Ask: *Which pair is better?* (the second) *Circle it.*

- Read aloud the sentence pairs for the second picture. Then say: *The first pair of sentences is about sitting next to a friend. It tells one good thing about lunchtime. The second pair of sentences is about eating lunch and dinner. It doesn't tell anything about the meals.* Ask: *Which is better?* (the first pair) *Circle it.*

Convention: Read the rule and the sentence aloud. Then point out the spaces between the words in the sentence. After students trace the sentence, have them point to each space between the words.

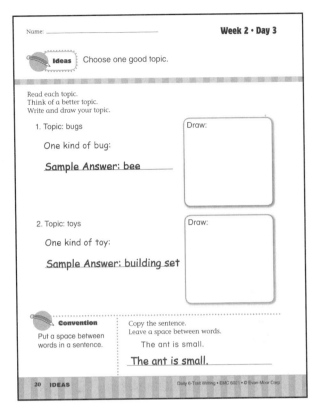

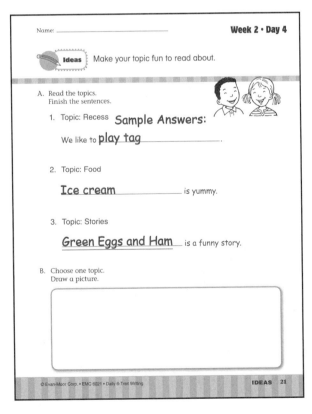

Read the rule aloud. Explain that today the class will be thinking of some good topics to write about. Then guide students through the activities. For example:

- Say: *Let's pretend we're going to write about bugs. There are many kinds of bugs.* Invite students to name different kinds, such as bees, spiders, ants, etc. Then say: *There are a lot of bugs! We can't write about them all. Let's pick one kind.*

- As a class, choose one kind of bug to write about and draw. Write the name of the bug on the board for students to copy. Repeat the process for the topic of toys in item 2.

Convention: Model copying the sentence onto a piece of paper. Model using your finger to gauge the right amount of space to leave between words.

Read the rule aloud. Explain that today the class will be thinking about good topics to write about. Then guide students through the activities. For example:

- **Activity A:** For item 1, read the topic and sentence aloud. Ask: *What do we like to do at recess? What is fun?* As a class, choose a recess activity. Write the activity on the board and have students copy it onto the blank line. Repeat the process for items 2 and 3.

- **Activity B:** As a class, choose one topic to write about on Day 5. Ask: *Which topic will be more fun to read about?* Have students circle that topic on their paper and illustrate it in the box.

DAY 5 *Writing Prompt*

- Have the class help you form an additional sentence about the topic they chose on Day 4. Have students copy both sentences.

- Remind students to leave a space between each word in their sentences.

 **Ideas** A good topic is fun to read about.

Which topic is more fun to read about?
Copy it.

milk

milk and cookies

1. Fun topic: _____

splash

rain

2. Fun topic: _____

 **Ideas**   A good topic is fun to read about.

Look at the picture.
Read the sentence pairs.
Which pair is more fun to read?

 1

a. We go to the park.
    We see trees.

b. We play ball at the park.
    Emma's team wins.

 2

a. Lunch is great.
    I sit by Billy.

b. I eat lunch.
    I eat dinner.

 Convention

Put a space between words in a sentence.

Trace this sentence.

We play ball.

 **Ideas** Choose one good topic.

Read each topic.
Think of a better topic.
Write and draw your topic.

1. Topic: bugs

   One kind of bug:

   _____

   Draw:

2. Topic: toys

   One kind of toy:

   _____

   Draw:

 **Convention**

Put a space between words in a sentence.

Copy the sentence.
Leave a space between words.

   The ant is small.

   _____

Ideas   Make your topic fun to read about.

A. Read the topics.
   Finish the sentences.

   1. Topic: Recess

       We like to _____ .

   2. Topic: Food

       _____ is yummy.

   3. Topic: Stories

       _____ is a funny story.

B. Choose one topic.
   Draw a picture.

   ┌──┐
   │   │
   │   │
   │   │
   │   │
   │   │
   └──┘

DAY 1

Read the rule aloud to introduce students to the concept of details. Then guide students through the activities. For example:

- **Activity A:** Write the word **detail** on the board. Say the word aloud and have students repeat after you. Then have students trace the word.

- **Activity B:** After reading the sentences for item 1, ask: *What do the sentences say about Ally?* (She is a friend; she has long hair; she smiles.) Say: *These are details about Ally.* Then guide students in reading and underlining the words that tell about these details. Repeat the process for item 2.

Convention: Read the rule aloud. Have students point to the first letter of each name as you read it aloud. Then have them trace the capital letter.

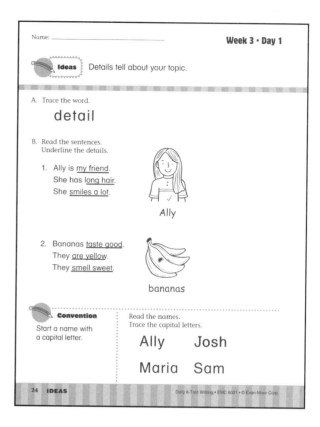

DAY 2

Read the rule aloud and remind students what a detail is. Then guide students through the activities. For example:

- **Activity A:** Direct students to the picture before reading the questions aloud. For question 1, model thinking through the answer. Say: *It looks like Ted spilled his cereal! Is he happy or sad?* (sad) Repeat the process for questions 2 and 3, writing the answers on the board for students to copy.

- **Activity B:** Ask: *What is one thing that Ted has?* Return to questions 1–3 to find possible answers. (e.g., hat, sad face, bowl) Then copy the sentence frame onto the board and model finishing it. For example: *Ted has a sad face.* Have students complete their sentence frames accordingly.

Convention: Read the rule and the sentence aloud. Then read Ted's name aloud as students trace over it. Then have them point to and circle the capital letter.

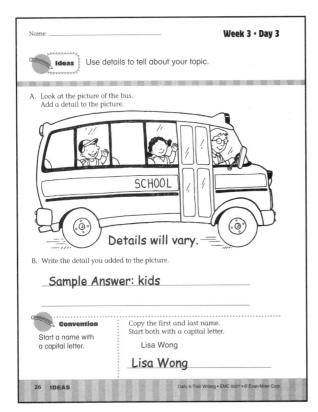

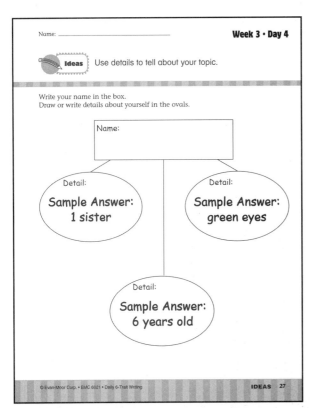

Read the rule aloud. Then guide students through the activities. For example:

- **Activity A:** Point to the bus and lead students in brainstorming details in the picture, such as wheels, windows, doors, driver, kids. Then ask: *What detail could we add to the picture?* (e.g., more kids in the windows) Have students add the detail to their pictures.

- **Activity B:** Say: *We drew (detail) in the picture. That is the detail we added.* Then write the word on the board for students to copy.

Convention: Remind students of the rule. Point out the first and last name as you read them aloud. Have students copy them.

Read the rule aloud and explain that today, students will think about details that describe themselves. Then guide students through the activity. For example:

- Copy the web onto the board. Say: *This is a web. We put our topic at the top. We put details about the topic in the ovals underneath.*

- Have students write their names in the box. Say: *You are the topic. Now, let's think of details about you. You could say how old you are, where you live, or what color hair you have.* Write some general details on the board for students to copy. (e.g., 6 years old; brown hair) Model writing the details in the appropriate parts of the web. Circulate and assist students as they fill in their webs.

DAY 5 *Writing Prompt*

- Post this sentence starter: *My name is ___.* Model filling it in with your name. Then post another starter, such as *I am ___ years old.* or *I have ___.* Have students copy the starters and fill them in with their names and details from their webs.

- Remind students to begin their names with a capital letter.

Ideas Details tell about your topic.

A. Trace the word.

detail

B. Read the sentences.
   Underline the details.

   1. Ally is my friend.
      She has long hair.
      She smiles a lot.

Ally

   2. Bananas taste good.
      They are yellow.
      They smell sweet.

bananas

Convention

Start a name with
a capital letter.

Read the names.
Trace the capital letters.

Ally   Josh

Maria   Sam

 **Ideas**   Use details to tell about your topic.

A. Look at the picture of Ted.
   Answer the questions about him.

   1. Is Ted happy or sad?

   2. What is on Ted's head?

   3. What is in Ted's hands?

      _____

B. Finish the sentence.

   Ted has a _____.

 Convention

Start a name with
a capital letter.

Trace the name. Circle the capital letter.

I see Ted.

 **Ideas** Use details to tell about your topic.

A. Look at the picture of the bus.
Add a detail to the picture.

SCHOOL

B. Write the detail you added to the picture.

_____

_____

 Convention

Start a name with
a capital letter.

Copy the first and last name.
Start both with a capital letter.

Lisa Wong

_____

 **Ideas** Use details to tell about your topic.

Write your name in the box.
Draw or write details about yourself in the ovals.

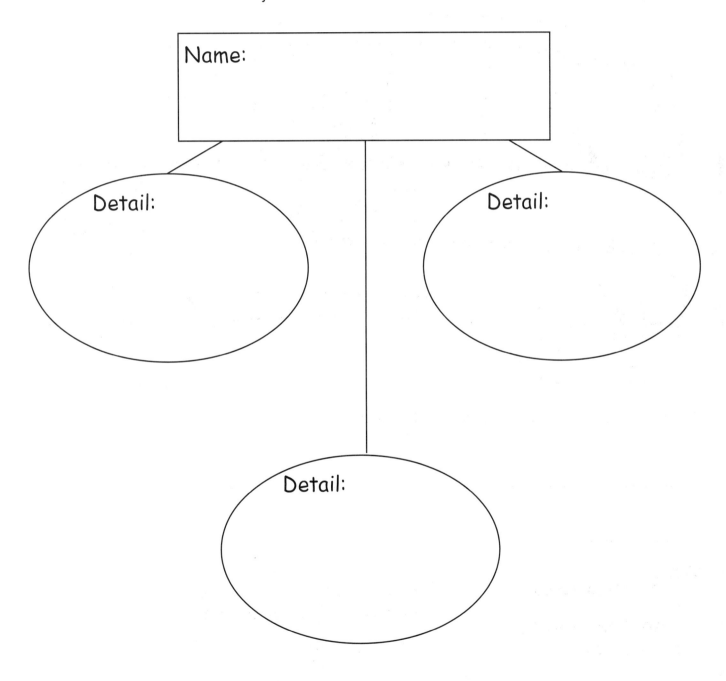

DAY 1

Review the meaning of **detail** from the previous week. Then read the rule aloud and explain that this week, students will learn how to choose the best details to make their writing better. Guide students through the activities. For example:

- **Activity A:** After reading each sentence aloud, ask: *Which sentences are exciting? Which ones help you picture what happened at the park?* Explain that while sentences 1 and 4 give important information, sentences 2 and 3 help the reader understand what was fun about Ocean Park.

- **Activity B:** After reading each sentence aloud, ask: *Which sentence tells about something interesting the author did at Ocean Park?* (the first sentence) Say: *That makes it a good detail.*

Convention: Read the rule and directions aloud. Then point out the first word. Say: ***Whales** is a naming word. It tells about more than one whale, so there is an **s** at the end. Circle the **s**.*

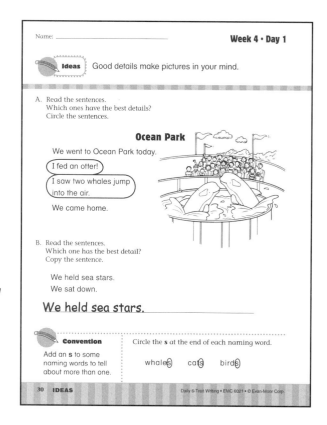

DAY 2

Read the rule aloud and explain that today, students will talk more about choosing good details. Then guide students through the activities. For example:

- Read each sentence and briefly explain how it gives interesting details about the fair. Say: *Games are something special you can do at the fair. If you win a game, you get a prize. You can also eat different kinds of food at the fair, like hot dogs.*

- Point out the picture and ask: *What are the kids doing?* (riding a ride) Have students help you form a sentence about the picture, starting with "You can," such as "You can go on rides." Write the sentence on the board for students to copy.

Convention: Read the rule and directions aloud. Then point to each singular noun and read it aloud as students fill in the **s**. Then read the new plural nouns and have students repeat after you.

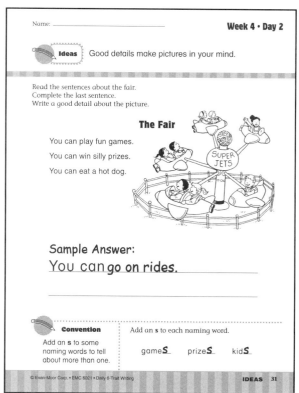

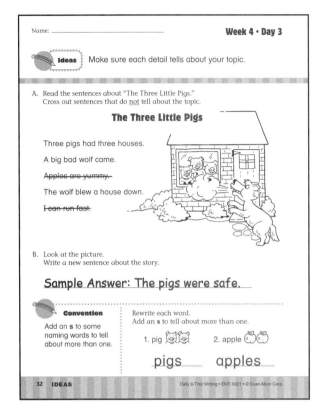

Name: _____ Week 4 • Day 3

Ideas Make sure each detail tells about your topic.

A. Read the sentences about "The Three Little Pigs."
Cross out sentences that do <u>not</u> tell about the topic.

The Three Little Pigs

Three pigs had three houses.

A big bad wolf came.

~~Apples are yummy.~~

The wolf blew a house down.

~~I can run fast.~~

B. Look at the picture.
Write a new sentence about the story.

Sample Answer: The pigs were safe.

Convention

Add an **s** to some naming words to tell about more than one.

Rewrite each word.
Add an **s** to tell about more than one.

1. pig   2. apple

    pigs   **apples**

32 IDEAS   Daily 6-Trait Writing • EMC 6021 • © Evan-Moor Corp.

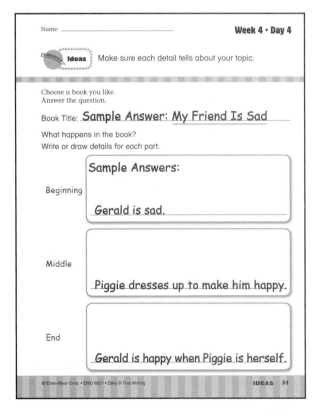

Name: _____ Week 4 • Day 4

Ideas Make sure each detail tells about your topic.

Choose a book you like.
Answer the question.

Book Title: **Sample Answer: My Friend Is Sad**

What happens in the book?
Write or draw details for each part.

Beginning

Sample Answers:

Gerald is sad.

Middle

Piggie dresses up to make him happy.

End

Gerald is happy when Piggie is herself.

© Evan-Moor Corp. • EMC 6021 • Daily 6-Trait Writing   IDEAS 33

DAY 3

Read the rule aloud and explain that details should always go with the topic. Then guide students through the activities. For example:

- **Activity A:** If necessary, review the story of "The Three Little Pigs." (A big bad wolf comes along and tries to blow down three pigs' houses made of straw, wood, and bricks.) Read aloud the first sentence and ask: *Does this sentence tell about the story?* (yes) Repeat the process for each item. For sentences 3 and 5, explain that while they may be true, they don't go with the story. Those sentences should be crossed out.

- **Activity B:** Point out the picture and ask: *What other detail could we tell about the story?* Gather ideas and choose one to write a sentence about, such as "The pigs were safe." Write the sentence on the board for students to copy.

Convention: Read the rule aloud. Then read item 1 and ask: *How many pigs are there?* (two) Say: *There is more than one pig, so we add an s to **pig**.* Have students write the plural word. Repeat for item 2.

DAY 4

Read the rule aloud. Then guide students through the activity. For example:

- As a class, choose a favorite book to write about. Write the title on the board for students to copy.

- Brainstorm what happens at the beginning, middle, and end of the book. With students' help, choose words that give details about what happens in each part of the book. Write them on the board for students to copy. Have students illustrate the details in the space provided.

DAY 5 *Writing Prompt*

- As a class, form a sentence that tells a good detail about the story chosen on Day 4. Have students copy the sentence from the board. Then have students write their own detail sentence.

- Encourage students to think of plural nouns that end with **s** to include in the sentence.

 **Ideas** Good details make pictures in your mind.

A. Read the sentences.
Which ones have the best details?
Circle the sentences.

Ocean Park

We went to Ocean Park today.

I fed an otter!

I saw two whales jump into the air.

We came home.

B. Read the sentences.
Which one has the best detail?
Copy the sentence.

We held sea stars.
We sat down.

_____

 Convention

Add an **s** to some naming words to tell about more than one.

Circle the **s** at the end of each naming word.

whales   cats   birds

 **Ideas**   Good details make pictures in your mind.

Read the sentences about the fair.
Complete the last sentence.
Write a good detail about the picture.

The Fair

You can play fun games.

You can win silly prizes.

You can eat a hot dog.

You can _____

_____

 Convention

Add an **s** to some naming words to tell about more than one.

Add an **s** to each naming word.

game__   prize__   kid__

Ideas ┊ Make sure each detail tells about your topic.

A. Read the sentences about "The Three Little Pigs."
   Cross out sentences that do <u>not</u> tell about the topic.

The Three Little Pigs

Three pigs had three houses.

A big bad wolf came.

Apples are yummy.

The wolf blew a house down.

I can run fast.

B. Look at the picture.
   Write a new sentence about the story.

_____

Convention

Add an **s** to some naming words to tell about more than one.

Rewrite each word.
Add an **s** to tell about more than one.

1. pig 🐷🐷   2. apple 🍎🍎

_____   _____

 **Ideas** Make sure each detail tells about your topic.

Choose a book you like.
Answer the question.

Book Title: _____

What happens in the book?
Write or draw details for each part.

Beginning

Middle

End

DAY 1

Read the rule aloud and review the term **topic**. Remind students that it is important to choose a topic before writing. Then guide students through the activities. For example:

- **Activity A:** After pointing to each picture and reading aloud its label, ask: *Which animal do you like the best?* Have students circle their choices.

- **Activity B:** Say: *The animal you just circled is your topic.* Read aloud the sentence frame and have students complete it with their topics. For example: *I can write about a frog.*

Convention: After reading the rule aloud, say: *This week, we'll practice writing the word **I**.* Have students trace over the letters. Then have them repeat after you as you read the completed sentences aloud.

Name: _____   Week 5 • Day 1

Ideas   Choose a topic before you write.

A. Read the animal topics.
   Choose one to write about.
   Circle the word.

   lion   zebra   frog

   Answers will vary.

B. Finish the sentence.

   I can write about a _____

Convention
Use a capital I to tell about yourself.

Trace each capital I.

   I have a fish.
   I feed my fish.

36   IDEAS   Daily 6-Trait Writing • EMC 6021 • © Evan-Moor Corp.

DAY 2

Read the rule aloud and explain that today, students will think of sports topics. Then guide students through the activities. For example:

- Say: *Pretend you are going to write about sports. There are many sports to write about!* Invite students to name sports they know. Choose three and list them on the board.

- Have students copy the name of each sport and/or draw something related to it in a box. For example, a basketball can represent the game of basketball.

- Read aloud the question and take a class vote on the best of the three sports. Tally the results and have students copy the name of the sport.

Convention: Read the rule aloud. Have students complete the sentences with capital **I**'s. Then have them repeat after you as you read the completed sentences aloud.

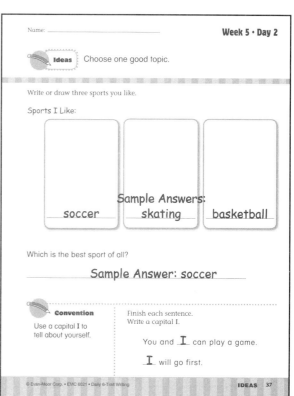

Name: _____   Week 5 • Day 2

Ideas   Choose one good topic.

Write or draw three sports you like.

Sports I Like:

                              Sample Answers:
   soccer   skating   basketball

Which is the best sport of all?

_____ Sample Answer: soccer _____

Convention
Use a capital I to tell about yourself.

Finish each sentence.
Write a capital I.

   You and I can play a game.

   I will go first.

© Evan-Moor Corp. • EMC 6021 • Daily 6-Trait Writing   IDEAS   37

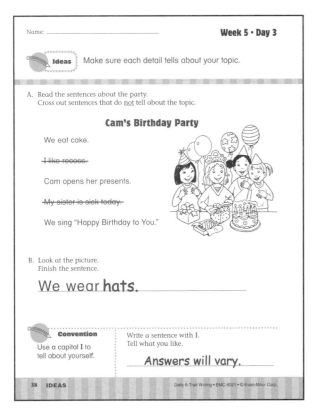

Read the rule aloud and briefly review the term **detail**. Then guide students through the activities. For example:

- **Activity A:** Ask: *Have you ever been to a birthday party?* Then read the title and the first sentence aloud. Ask: *Does this sentence tell about the topic "a birthday party"?* (yes) Repeat the process for each sentence. Explain that while sentences 2 and 4 may be true, they don't go with the topic.

- **Activity B:** Say: *Let's add a detail to the story.* Ask: *What are the kids wearing in the picture?* (hats) Then read the sentence frame aloud. Ask: *What word can finish the sentence?* (**hats**) Write the word on the board and have students copy it. Then read the completed sentence aloud in unison.

Convention: Review the rule. Then ask: *What do you like about parties?* Write responses on the board. Model how to construct a sentence, such as "I like presents."

DAY 4

Read the rule aloud. Then guide students through the activities. For example:

- **Activity A:** Say: *Yesterday, we read about a birthday party. Today, let's think of a party we've been to.* Help students think of and choose a party. Then help students brainstorm details to include, such as people, food, decorations, etc.

- **Activity B:** Ask: *What are your favorite details that you drew?* Invite volunteers to share their favorites. Write a few key words on the board. Have students circle their favorite details in their drawings and copy or write words that describe them, such as **music**, **games**, or **cake**.

DAY 5 *Writing Prompt*

- Write sentence frames on the board, such as *I saw ___. I liked ___.* Then have students copy the frames and fill them in with their favorite details from Day 4.

- Remind students to use a capital **I** in each sentence.

 **Ideas** Choose a topic before you write.

A. Read the animal topics.
    Choose one to write about.
    Circle the word.

lion   zebra   frog

B. Finish the sentence.

I can write about a _____

 **Convention**

Use a capital **I** to
tell about yourself.

Trace each capital **I**.

I have a fish.

I feed my fish.

 **Ideas** Choose one good topic.

Write or draw three sports you like.

Sports I Like:

Which is the best sport of all?

_____

 **Convention**

Use a capital **I** to tell about yourself.

Finish each sentence.
Write a capital **I**.

You and ___ can play a game.

___ will go first.

 **Ideas** Make sure each detail tells about your topic.

A. Read the sentences about the party.
    Cross out sentences that do <u>not</u> tell about the topic.

Cam's Birthday Party

We eat cake.

I like recess.

Cam opens her presents.

My sister is sick today.

We sing "Happy Birthday to You."

B. Look at the picture.
    Finish the sentence.

We wear _____

 Convention

Use a capital **I** to tell about yourself.

Write a sentence with **I**.
Tell what you like.

_____

 **Ideas** Use good details to tell about your topic.

A. Draw a picture of a party.
   Draw as many details as you can.

B. Circle two good details in your drawing.
   Write them below.

_____   _____

ORGANIZATION
Beginning, Middle, and End

Refer to pages 6 and 7 to introduce or review the writing trait.

DAY 1

Read the rule aloud to introduce the idea that a story has three parts. Then guide students through the activities. For example:

- Read the story title. Then have students look at each picture in order as you read aloud the story. Return to the first picture and say: *This is the beginning of the story. It's where the story starts.* Ask: *What does the beginning tell us?* (that Jill has a new hat) Have students trace over the word **beginning** and draw a line from the picture to the word.

- Repeat the process for the second and third pictures. For the second picture, say: *This is the middle of the story. The middle comes after the beginning.* Ask: *What happens in the middle?* (Jill's hat blows away.) For the third picture, say: *This is the end of the story. It is the last part.* Ask: *How does the story end?* (The hat lands on the snowman.)

Convention: Review the rule. Read the sentence aloud and point to the letter choices. Ask: *Should the sentence start with a capital **T** or a small **t**?* (capital **T**)

DAY 2

Read the rule aloud. Then guide students through the activities. For example:

- **Activity A:** Read the story title. Write the words **beginning**, **middle**, and **end** on the board. Guide students to label the pictures in order. Then point to the first picture and ask: *What is Sam doing in the beginning?* (He is counting.) For the second picture, ask: *What is Sam doing in the middle?* (He is looking around.) For the third picture, ask: *What does Jen do in the end?* (She comes out from behind the tree.)

- **Activity B:** Read the first sentence. Ask: *Where did we see Jen—in the beginning, middle, or end?* (end) Have students draw a line from the sentence to **end**. Repeat the process for each sentence.

Convention: Review the rule. Read aloud each name as students complete the activity.

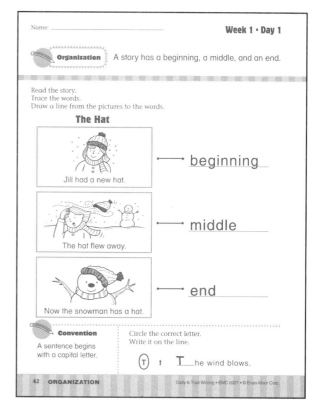

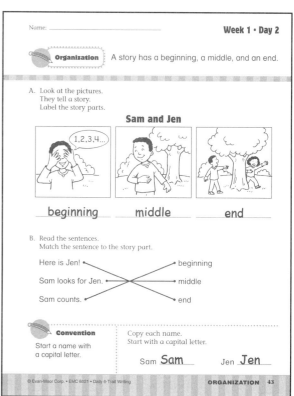

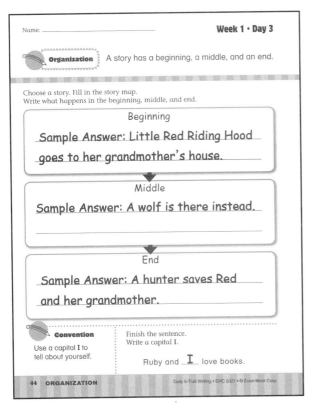

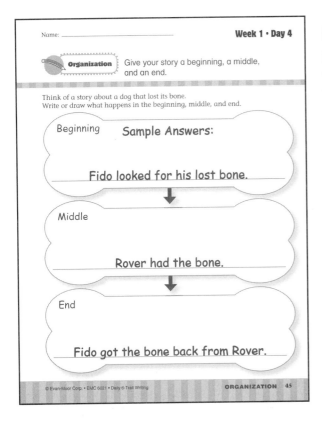

Read the rule aloud. Then guide students through the activities. For example:

- Copy the story map onto the board. Point to the map and say: *This is a story map. You fill it in to tell what happens in the beginning, middle, and end.*

- As a class, choose a story that students are familiar with. Then invite volunteers to tell what happens in the beginning, middle, and end of the story. Jot notes on the story map. If students retell events out of order, use the parts of the story map to clarify what happened when.

- Have students help you form a sentence to tell what happens in the beginning of the story. Write the sentence on the board for students to copy onto their own maps. Repeat for the middle and end of the story.

Convention: Read the rule. Then read aloud the sentence before having students complete it with a capital **I**.

DAY 4

Read the rule aloud. Explain that today, students will create a story of their own. Then guide students through the activity. For example:

- As a class, brainstorm a story about a dog that lost its bone. Use questions to prompt students, such as: *What is the dog's name? Where did he or she lose the bone? How was it found?*

- Help students work out what happens in the beginning, middle, and end of their own story. Then direct them to draw or write what happens in each part.

DAY 5 *Writing Prompt*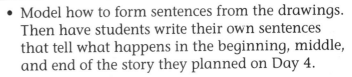

- Model how to form sentences from the drawings. Then have students write their own sentences that tell what happens in the beginning, middle, and end of the story they planned on Day 4.

- Remind students to capitalize sentences, names, and the word **I**.

Name: _____

 **Organization** A story has a beginning, a middle, and an end.

Read the story.
Trace the words.
Draw a line from the pictures to the words.

The Hat

Jill had a new hat.

•   • beginning

The hat flew away.

•   • middle

Now the snowman has a hat.

•   • end

 Convention

A sentence begins
with a capital letter.

Circle the correct letter.
Write it on the line.

T   t   _____he wind blows.

 **Organization**   A story has a beginning, a middle, and an end.

A. Look at the pictures.
   They tell a story.
   Label the story parts.

Sam and Jen

_____   _____   _____

B. Read the sentences.
   Match the sentence to the story part.

Here is Jen! •   • beginning

Sam looks for Jen. •   • middle

Sam counts. •   • end

 Convention

Start a name with
a capital letter.

Copy each name.
Start with a capital letter.

Sam _____   Jen _____

Name: _____

 **Organization** : A story has a beginning, a middle, and an end.

Choose a story. Fill in the story map.
Write what happens in the beginning, middle, and end.

Beginning

_____

_____

Middle

_____

_____

End

_____

_____

Convention

Use a capital **I** to tell about yourself.

Finish the sentence.
Write a capital **I**.

Ruby and _____ love books.

 **Organization**   Give your story a beginning, a middle, and an end.

Think of a story about a dog that lost its bone.
Write or draw what happens in the beginning, middle, and end.

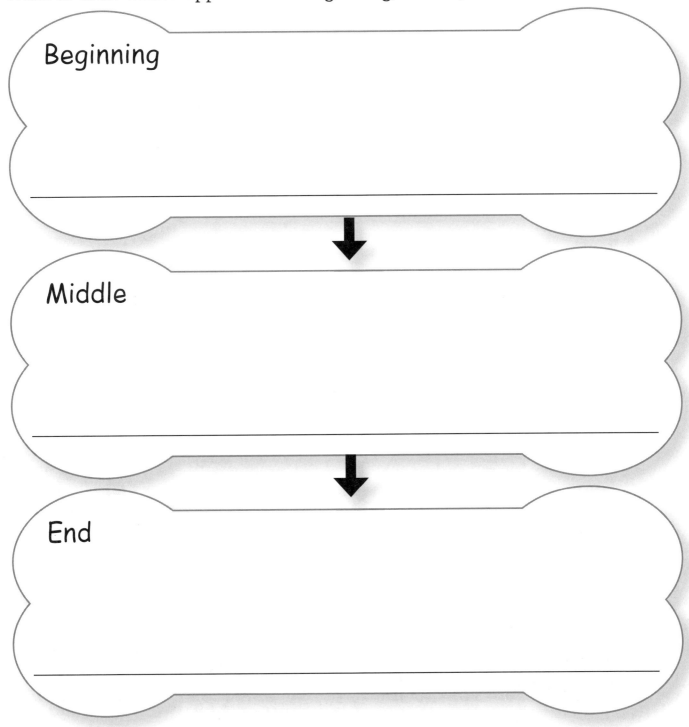

Beginning

Middle

End

ORGANIZATION
Put Things in the Right Order

DAY 1

Read the rule aloud and say: *Last week, we learned how a story goes from the beginning to the middle to the end. We call this going in the right order. This week, we'll learn more about putting our writing in the right order.* Then guide students through the activities. For example:

- **Activity A:** Say: *When you put things in order, you put each thing in the right place.* Then read the story aloud. Check for understanding by asking: *What did Dino do first? What did Dino do last?* Say: *This is the order that Dino did things.*

- **Activity B:** Have students follow along as you read each sentence. Help students determine the order of the sentences, explaining that words such as **first** and **then** give clues to order.

Convention: Read the rule. Then read the sample sentence. Ask: *Can you find the period at the end of the sentence?* Have students point to and circle the period in the sentence.

DAY 2

Read the rule aloud. Remind students what **order** is and why it is important. Then guide them through the activities. For example:

- Have students look at each picture and describe what they see.

- Read the words in the box and explain that students will add each word to a sentence to tell the order of what happened in the pictures.

- Read the first sentence aloud and ask: *Does this sentence tell what happened in the beginning, middle, or end of the story?* (beginning) *Which word in the word box tells what happens in the beginning?* (**First**) Have students complete the sentence with **First**.

- Repeat the process for each sentence, explaining that **next** and **then** can both signal what happens in the middle of a story.

Convention: Read the rule and the sentence aloud. Then ask: *Can you place the period at the end of the sentence?* Have students place the period on the line.

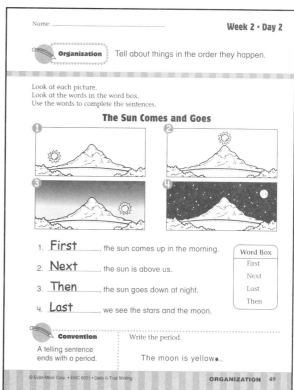

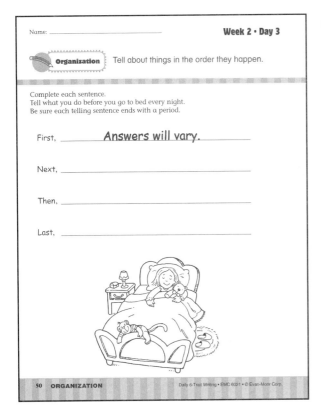

Name: _____   **Week 2 • Day 3**

Organization   Tell about things in the order they happen.

Complete each sentence.
Tell what you do before you go to bed every night.
Be sure each telling sentence ends with a period.

First, _____**Answers will vary.**_____

Next, _____

Then, _____

Last, _____

50   ORGANIZATION   Daily 6-Trait Writing • EMC 6021 • © Evan-Moor Corp.

Name: _____   **Week 2 • Day 4**

Organization   Tell about things in the order they happen.

Think of four things you do before you go to school.
Draw them in the correct order.

① First

Drawings will vary, but should be in the correct order.

② Next

③ Then

④ Last

© Evan-Moor Corp. • EMC 6021 • Daily 6-Trait Writing   ORGANIZATION   51

DAY 3

Read the rule aloud. Then guide students through the activity. For example:

- Help students brainstorm pre-bedtime activities. (brushing their teeth, putting on pajamas, reading a story, saying goodnight)

- Point to the first sentence and have students read the first word with you. Say: *The sentence starts with the word* **First**, *so let's write a sentence about what we do first.* Have students suggest a sentence for you to write on the board. (e.g., "First, I put on my pajamas.") Then have students copy the sentence onto their own papers.

- Repeat the process for the other sentences.

Convention: Point out the periods in the sentences you wrote. Have students check their own sentences to make sure they end with a period.

DAY 4

Read the rule aloud. Then guide students through the activity. For example:

- Help students brainstorm morning activities. Model choosing four things you do before school and involve students in figuring out the order. (wake up, get dressed, eat breakfast, brush teeth)

- Use a think-aloud to model completing the drawings. Say: *Box 1 has the word* **First** *in it. I'll draw what I do first here.* As you draw, emphasize that you are drawing just to show your idea and that details are not necessary. For example, a toothbrush could represent brushing your teeth.

DAY 5 *Writing Prompt*

- Have students use their drawings from Day 4 to write four sentences that tell what they do before school in the morning. You may wish to do this as a group.

- Remind students to end each telling sentence with a period.

 **Organization** Tell about things in the order they happen.

A. Read the story.
   Look at each picture.

Dino's Day

①
First, Dino eats his lunch.

②
Next, Dino takes a nap.

③
Then, Dino waits for Nick.

④
Last, Dino goes for a walk!

B. Read these sentences.
   Number them in the correct order.

____ Then, Dino waits for Nick.   ____ Next, Dino takes a nap.

____ Last, Dino goes for a walk!   ____ First, Dino eats his lunch.

 Convention   Circle the period in the sentence.

A telling sentence
ends with a period.   Dino loves Nick.

 **Organization**   Tell about things in the order they happen.

Look at each picture.
Look at the words in the word box.
Use the words to complete the sentences.

The Sun Comes and Goes

1. _____, the sun comes up in the morning.

2. _____, the sun is above us.

3. _____, the sun goes down at night.

4. _____, we see the stars and the moon.

Word Box
First
Next
Last
Then

 Convention

A telling sentence
ends with a period.

Write the period.

The moon is yellow___

 **Organization**   Tell about things in the order they happen.

Complete each sentence.
Tell what you do before you go to bed every night.
Be sure each telling sentence ends with a period.

First, _____

Next, _____

Then, _____

Last, _____

Name: _____

 **Organization**   Tell about things in the order they happen.

Think of four things you do before you go to school.
Draw them in the correct order.

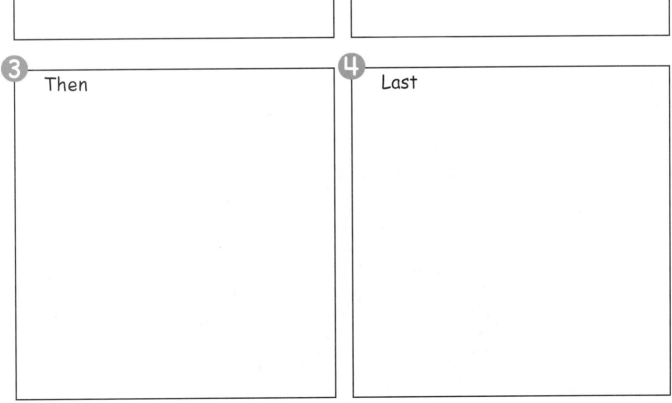

① First

② Next

③ Then

④ Last

ORGANIZATION
Write a Complete Ending

DAY 1

Review the parts of a story from Week 1. Then read the rule aloud and explain that this week, students will learn more about endings. Say: *There is more to an ending than just saying "The end."* Then guide students through the activities. For example:

- **Activity A:** After reading the story, check for understanding by asking: *Why is John sad?* Then read aloud the question. Prompt students by asking: *Don't you want to know what happens to John?* Explain that the end of the story is missing. Have students write **end** on the line.

- **Activity B:** Read aloud the answer choices. Then ask: *Which sentence tells what happens to John and Jess?* (the first) Explain that it is the better ending. The other choice only tells what Jess does.

Convention: Read the rule aloud. Write the words **to** and **two** on the board and have students repeat them after you. Explain what each word means. Then say: *We need to be careful when we spell these words.* Read the sentence aloud as students finish it.

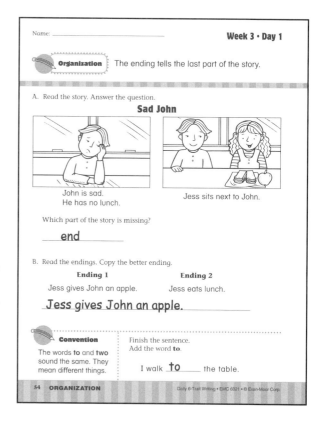

DAY 2

Read the rule aloud. Say: *Yesterday, we learned that stories need endings. But other kinds of writing need endings, too.* Then guide students through the activities. For example:

- If necessary, explain that a sandwich is two slices of bread with meat, or other foods, in between. Read the title aloud. Then have students echo you as you read steps 1–4.

- For step 5, ask: *What is the last thing you do? What goes on top of the sandwich?* (a piece of bread) Form a sentence that begins with **Put**, such as "Put a slice of bread on top," and write it on the board for students to copy.

Convention: Review the rule. Write the number **2** to clarify the meaning of **two**. Read the sentence aloud as students fill it in.

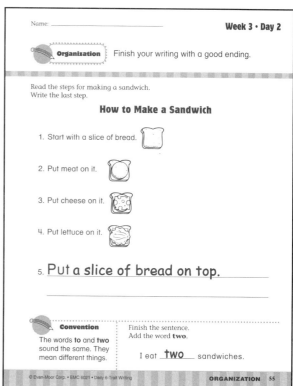

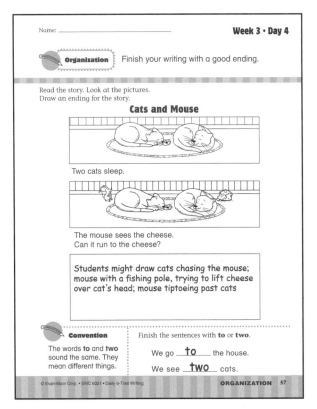

Read the rule aloud. Then guide students through the activity. For example:

- Point out Mama Bird and Baby Bird and their speech balloons. Say: *This is what they are saying.* Read the dialogue aloud.

- Prompt students to give a description of the story. For example, ask: *Where are the birds sitting? What is happening? Does Baby Bird look happy or scared?*

- Direct students to the third panel and say: *Baby Bird finally tried to fly!* Ask: *How do you think Mama Bird feels? What would she say in the end?* Invite students to give possibilities. Explain that the end should make sense with the rest of the story. Then choose one suggestion and write it on the board for students to copy.

DAY 4

Review the rule. Then guide students through the activities. For example:

- Read the sentences for the first two panels. Check for understanding by asking: *What is in between the mouse and the cheese? Why wouldn't the mouse want to wake up the cats?*

- Ask: *What do you think the mouse will do? Will it be brave and try to run past the cats? Will it go away hungry? What else could it do?* Invite students to give two or three suggestions, assessing whether they are logical conclusions to the story. Then have students choose an ending and draw it in the box.

Convention: Review what **to** and **two** mean. Then read aloud each sentence as students fill it in.

DAY 5 *Writing Prompt*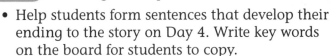

- Help students form sentences that develop their ending to the story on Day 4. Write key words on the board for students to copy.

- Remind students to spell **to** and **two** correctly.

Name: _____

 **Organization**   The ending tells the last part of the story.

A. Read the story. Answer the question.

Sad John

John is sad.
He has no lunch.

Jess sits next to John.

Which part of the story is missing?

_____

B. Read the endings. Copy the better ending.

Ending 1

Jess gives John an apple.

Ending 2

Jess eats lunch.

_____

 Convention

The words **to** and **two** sound the same. They mean different things.

Finish the sentence.
Add the word **to**.

I walk _____ the table.

Name: _____

 **Organization**   Finish your writing with a good ending.

Read the steps for making a sandwich.
Write the last step.

How to Make a Sandwich

1. Start with a slice of bread.

2. Put meat on it.

3. Put cheese on it.

4. Put lettuce on it.

5. Put _____

_____

 Convention

The words **to** and **two** sound the same. They mean different things.

Finish the sentence.
Add the word **two**.

I eat _____ sandwiches.

 **Organization** Finish your writing with a good ending.

Read the story.
Write what Mama Bird says in the end.

Baby Bird

Name: _____

Organization   Finish your writing with a good ending.

Read the story. Look at the pictures.
Draw an ending for the story.

Cats and Mouse

Two cats sleep.

The mouse sees the cheese.
Can it run to the cheese?

Convention

The words **to** and **two** sound the same. They mean different things.

Finish the sentences with **to** or **two**.

We go _____ the house.

We see _____ cats.

DAY 1

Read the rule aloud and explain that one way to write about two things is to tell how they are the same or different. Then guide students through the activities. For example:

- **Activity A:** Point to the two sheep. Say: *The two sheep look just like each other. They are the same.* Have students say the word and trace it. Repeat the process for item 2, saying: *The fish does not look like the sheep. They are different.*

- **Activity B:** Read item 1 aloud. Point to the pictures of the bears and ask: *Are they the same or different?* (same) Have students write **same** on the line. Repeat the process for item 2. For item 3, elicit that the truck has wheels, and the bear is a stuffed animal. Form a sentence on the board for students to copy onto their papers.

Convention: Display a calendar and point out that the months begin with capital letters. Read aloud each month in the activity as students trace over its letter.

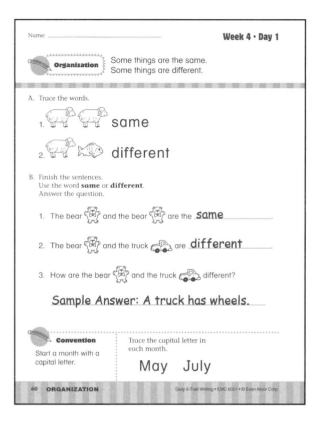

DAY 2

Read the rule aloud. Then guide students through the activities. For example:

- **Activity A:** Say: *Alike means two things are the same in some ways but different in others.* Use two students as an example. Say: *(Girl's name) and (girl's name) are girls. They are not exactly the same, but they are alike because they are both girls.* Have students say the word and trace it.

- **Activity B:** Read through item 1 and discuss how pizza and pie are alike. They are both round foods and have a crust. Have students circle the pizza and pie. Repeat the process for item 2.

- **Activity C:** Have students choose a pair of words from item 1 or 2 to complete the sentences. Model words on the board as necessary.

Convention: Display a calendar and point out that days of the week begin with capital letters. Read aloud each day in the activity as students trace over its letter.

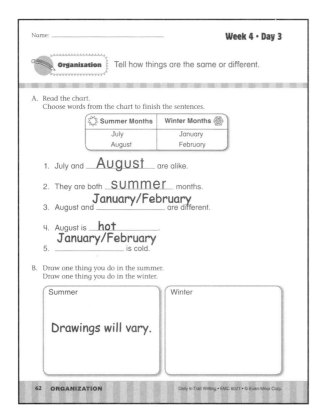

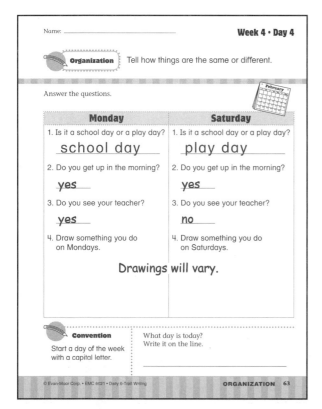

Read the rule aloud. Then guide students through the activities. For example:

- **Activity A:** If necessary, review the four seasons and what the weather is like in each one. Then point out the chart and say: *This chart tells you which season these months are in.* Read aloud item 1. Say: *July is a summer month.* Refer to the chart and ask: *Which month is like July?* (**August**) Have students trace the word. Continue to read aloud the sentences and use the chart to help students find the answers.

- **Activity B:** To get students started, brainstorm popular activities in your area during the summer and winter.

Read the rule aloud. Then guide students through the activities. For example:

- Briefly review the days of the week with students, emphasizing that Saturday and Sunday are weekends. Say: *Students don't normally go to school on those days. Many kids play on those days.*

- Point out the chart and explain that students will use it to compare Mondays and Saturdays by answering questions about these days. Read aloud question 1. Ask: *Is Monday a school day or a play day?* (school day) Have students trace over the answer. Then help students complete the remaining questions.

- Guide students through the Convention activity.

Writing Prompt

- Post these sentences: *Monday and Saturday are alike. Monday and Saturday are different.* Then have students use their charts from Day 4 to help you form a sentence that supports each statement. (e.g., On both days, we get up in the morning. But on Monday, we go to school. On Saturday, we play.) Have students copy the sentences onto their papers.

- Remind students to capitalize **Monday** and **Saturday**.

 **Organization**

Some things are the same.
Some things are different.

A. Trace the words.

1.    same

2.    different

B. Finish the sentences.
    Use the word **same** or **different**.
    Answer the question.

1. The bear and the bear are the _____.

2. The bear and the truck are _____.

3. How are the bear and the truck different?

    _____

Convention

Start a month with a
capital letter.

Trace the capital letter in
each month.

May   July

 **Organization**   Some things are alike.

A. Trace the word.

alike

B. Look at each group of pictures.
Circle the things that are **alike**.

1.   pizza   pie   bunny

2.   flower   truck   tree

C. Choose words to finish the sentences.

A _____ and a _____ are alike.

They are both _____.

 Convention

Start a day of the week
with a capital letter.

Trace the capital letter in each
day of the week.

Sunday   Friday

 **Organization**   Tell how things are the same or different.

A. Read the chart.
   Choose words from the chart to finish the sentences.

☀ Summer Months	Winter Months ❄
July	January
August	February

1. July and ___August___ are alike.

2. They are both ___summer___ months.

3. August and _____ are different.

4. August is _____.

5. _____ is cold.

B. Draw one thing you do in the summer.
   Draw one thing you do in the winter.

Summer	Winter

 **Organization** Tell how things are the same or different.

Answer the questions.

Monday	**Saturday**
1. Is it a school day or a play day? <u>school day</u>	1. Is it a school day or a play day? <u>play day</u>
2. Do you get up in the morning? _____	2. Do you get up in the morning? _____
3. Do you see your teacher? _____	3. Do you see your teacher? _____
4. Draw something you do on Mondays.	4. Draw something you do on Saturdays.

 Convention

Start a day of the week with a capital letter.

What day is today?
Write it on the line.

_____

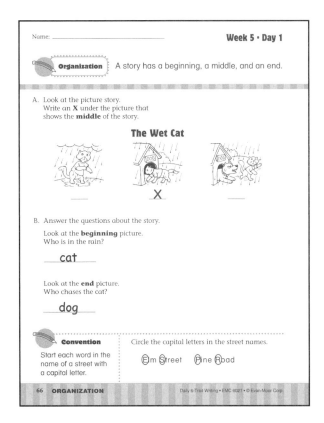

DAY 1

Read the rule aloud and review the parts of a story. Then guide students through the activities. For example:

- **Activity A:** Read the story title. Then point out the first picture and say: *It's raining! The cat is getting wet. He doesn't like that.* Point out the second picture and ask: *Where is the cat going?* (into a doghouse) Point out the third picture and ask: *What happens now?* (The dog is chasing the cat.) Ask: *Which picture shows the beginning? The middle? The end?* Then have students mark an **X** under the middle picture.

- **Activity B:** Read the first question. Have students point to the beginning picture. Then help them find the answer to the question and write it on the line. Repeat the process for the second question.

Convention: Read the rule aloud. Explain that a street can also be called **avenue**, **road**, **lane**, etc. Those words should also be capitalized when they are part of the name of a street. Read aloud the streets as students complete the activity.

DAY 2

Read the rule aloud. Then guide students through the activities. For example:

- **Activity A:** Point to the pictures and read the sentences aloud. Check for understanding by asking: *What did Holly do? How do you think she feels?*

- **Activity B:** Ask: *Now what do you think Holly will do? Will she tell someone what she did? What else could she do?* Invite students to give suggestions, reminding them they must be logical conclusions to the story. Then have them choose an ending and draw it in the box. Students may also write words or a sentence, depending upon their ability. You may want to write a few different sentences on the board for students to copy.

Convention: Review the rule. Then read aloud the sentence before students trace over the letters.

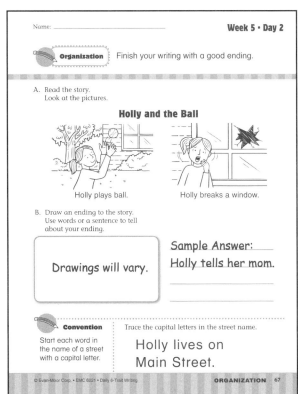

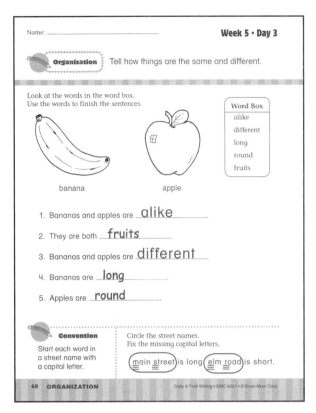

Name: _____   **Week 5 • Day 3**

Organization   Tell how things are the same and different.

Look at the words in the word box.
Use the words to finish the sentences.

Word Box
alike
different
long
round
fruits

banana   apple

1. Bananas and apples are _alike_
2. They are both _fruits_.
3. Bananas and apples are _different_
4. Bananas are _long_
5. Apples are _round_

Convention

Start each word in a street name with a capital letter.

Circle the street names.
Fix the missing capital letters.

main street is long   elm road is short.

68   **ORGANIZATION**   Daily 6-Trait Writing • EMC 6021 • © Evan-Moor Corp.

DAY 3

Read the rule aloud. Then guide students through the activities. For example:

- Point to the banana and apple. Say: *Today, we are going to tell how a banana and an apple are the same and how they are different.* Then read aloud the words in the box and have students repeat them. Read item 1. Have students trace over the word and echo you as you read the completed sentence aloud.

- Read item 2. Ask: *Which word tells how bananas and apples are alike?* (**fruits**) Have students write the word on the line and echo you as you read the completed sentence aloud. Repeat the process for items 3–5.

Convention: Review the rule. Read aloud the sentences and ask: *What are the street names? Which letters should be capitalized?* (**m, s, e, r**) Model using proofreading marks to indicate capitalization.

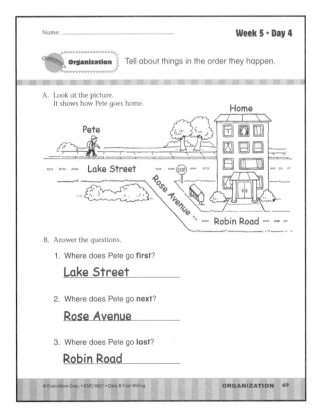

Name: _____   **Week 5 • Day 4**

Organization   Tell about things in the order they happen.

A. Look at the picture.
   It shows how Pete goes home.

Home

Pete

Lake Street

Rose Avenue

Robin Road

B. Answer the questions.

1. Where does Pete go **first**?
   Lake Street

2. Where does Pete go **next**?
   Rose Avenue

3. Where does Pete go **last**?
   Robin Road

© Evan-Moor Corp. • EMC 6021 • Daily 6-Trait Writing   **ORGANIZATION**   69

DAY 4

Read the rule aloud. Then guide students through the activities. For example:

- **Activity A:** Point to Pete and say: *This is Pete. This path shows how he gets home from school.* Then guide students from one end of Pete's walk to the other, reading aloud the street names.

- **Activity B:** Read aloud question 1. Have students point to the street Pete starts on. (**Lake Street**) Have students copy the street name onto the line, reminding them to start each word with a capital letter. Repeat for questions 2 and 3.

DAY 5   *Writing Prompt*

- Have students write three sentences that tell about Pete's route from Day 4. Each sentence should start with **First**, **Next**, or **Last**. You may wish to do this as a group.

- Remind students to capitalize each street name.

 **Organization**   A story has a beginning, a middle, and an end.

A. Look at the picture story.
    Write an **X** under the picture that
    shows the **middle** of the story.

The Wet Cat

_____   _____   _____

B. Answer the questions about the story.

Look at the **beginning** picture.
Who is in the rain?

_____

Look at the **end** picture.
Who chases the cat?

_____

Convention

Start each word in the
name of a street with
a capital letter.

Circle the capital letters in the street names.

Elm Street   Pine Road

 **Organization**   Finish your writing with a good ending.

A. Read the story.
    Look at the pictures.

Holly and the Ball

Holly plays ball.

Holly breaks a window.

B. Draw an ending to the story.
    Use words or a sentence to tell
    about your ending.

_____

_____

_____

_____

 Convention

Start each word in
the name of a street
with a capital letter.

Trace the capital letters in the street name.

Holly lives on
Main Street.

Name: _____

 **Organization** Tell how things are the same and different.

Look at the words in the word box.
Use the words to finish the sentences.

Word Box
alike
different
long
round
fruits

banana   apple

1. Bananas and apples are ___alike___.

2. They are both _____.

3. Bananas and apples are ___different___.

4. Bananas are _____.

5. Apples are _____.

 Convention

Start each word in
a street name with
a capital letter.

Circle the street names.
Fix the missing capital letters.

main street is long. elm road is short.

 **Organization**   Tell about things in the order they happen.

A. Look at the picture.
    It shows how Pete goes home.

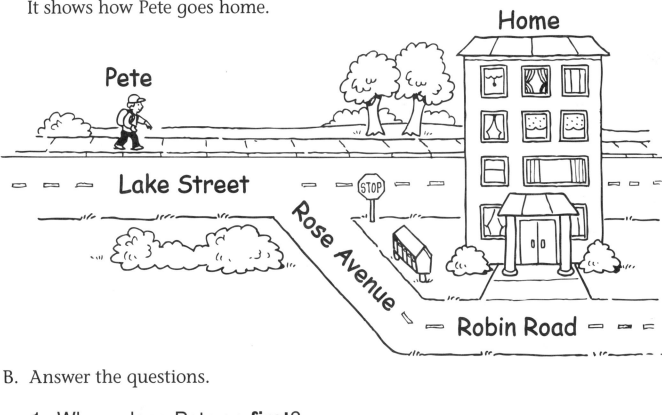

B. Answer the questions.

   1. Where does Pete go **first**?

      _____

   2. Where does Pete go **next**?

      _____

   3. Where does Pete go **last**?

      _____

WORD CHOICE
Use Action Words

Refer to pages 6 and 7 to introduce or review the writing trait.

DAY 1

Read the rule aloud and explain that an action is something that is happening. It is what someone or something does. Then guide students through the activities. For example:

- Have students repeat after you as you read each word in the word box. Say: *These are all things that someone or something can do. They are actions. Let's choose the right action for each picture.*

- Point to item 1. Ask: *What is the dog doing?* (digging) Say: *Point to the word **dig** in the word box.* Then have students trace the word **dig** on the line. Repeat the process for items 2–6, but have students write the word from the box on the line.

Convention: Read the rule. Say: *You use an asking sentence when you want to ask a question. For example, "What's your name?" is an asking sentence.* Read the question aloud and have students repeat after you. Ask: *What is the sentence asking?* (whether or not you can swim) Say: *An asking sentence always ends with a question mark. Can you find the question mark at the end of the sentence?* Have students point to it and circle it.

DAY 2

Read the rule aloud. Then guide students through the activities. For example:

- **Activity A:** Point out the sentences and say: *These sentences tell about what's happening in the picture. Every sentence has an action word. Let's find each one.* Read aloud the first sentence. Have students point out the corresponding action in the picture. Ask: *Which word in this sentence tells about the action?* (**runs**) *Runs is the action word.* Have students trace over the circle. Repeat the process for items 2–4.

- **Activity B:** Read aloud the words in the word box and have students repeat after you. Then read item 1. Ask: *Which action word fits the sentence?* (**jump**) Have students copy the word onto the line and read the completed sentence aloud. Repeat the process for items 2 and 3.

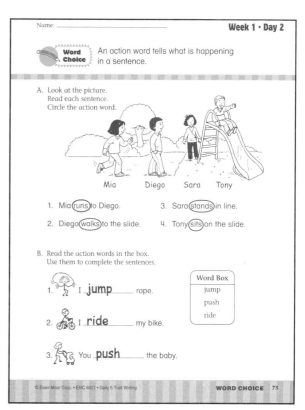

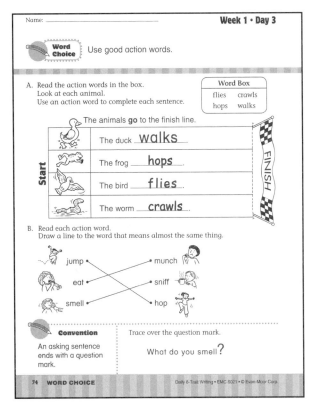

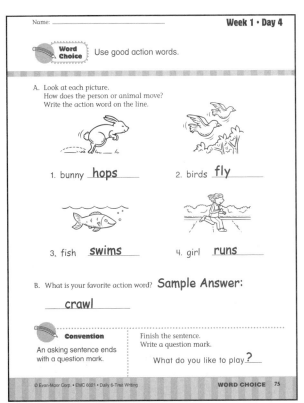

DAY 3

Read the rule aloud. Then guide students through the activities. For example:

- **Activity A:** Read the top sentence. Say: *Go is an okay action word. But there are many ways to tell how we go someplace. These animals are in a race. Let's choose the word that tells exactly how they go to the finish line.* Read aloud each word in the box and have students repeat after you. Read the first sentence and ask: *Which word tells how the duck goes?* (**walks**) Have students trace over the word. Repeat the process for the remaining sentences.

- **Activity B:** Say: *Some action words mean almost the same thing.* Read aloud each word in Activity B. Then point out **jump.** Ask: *Which other word is like jump?* (**hop**) Have students draw a line from one to the other. Repeat for the remaining items.

Convention: Review the rule. Read the question aloud before students complete the activity.

DAY 4

Review the rule. Then guide students through the activities. For example:

- **Activity A:** For item 1, say: *Look at the bunny. How does this bunny move?* (**hops**) If necessary, write the word on the board for students to copy. Repeat for items 2–4.

- **Activity B:** Invite students to tell the best action words they've learned during the week.

Convention: Review the rule. Read the sentence aloud before students complete the activity.

DAY 5 *Writing Prompt*

- Post these frames: *What can a ___ do? A ___ can ___.* Model filling them in, using an animal and action word from Day 4. (What can a bunny do? A bunny can hop.) Have students copy the frames to write about three animals, using words from Days 1–4.

- Remind students to put a question mark at the end of the asking sentence.

 **Word Choice** Action words tell what people or things do.

Read the action words in the box.
Look at each picture.
Write the action word on the line.

Word Box		
run	fall	rest
dig	lick	swim

1. ___dig___

2. _____

3. _____

4. _____

5. _____

6. _____

 Convention

An asking sentence
ends with a
question mark.

Circle the question mark.

Can you swim?

Name: _____

 **Word Choice** An action word tells what is happening in a sentence.

A. Look at the picture.
Read each sentence.
Circle the action word.

Mia   Diego   Sara   Tony

1. Mia (runs) to Diego.

2. Diego walks to the slide.

3. Sara stands in line.

4. Tony sits on the slide.

B. Read the action words in the box.
Use them to complete the sentences.

 1. I _____ rope.

 2. I _____ my bike.

 3. You _____ the baby.

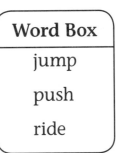

Word Box

jump

push

ride

 **Word Choice**   Use good action words.

A. Read the action words in the box.
Look at each animal.
Use an action word to complete each sentence.

Word Box	
flies	crawls
hops	walks

The animals **go** to the finish line.

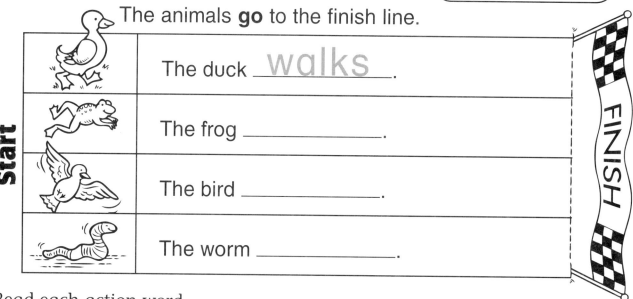

The duck ___walks___.

The frog _____.

The bird _____.

The worm _____.

B. Read each action word.
Draw a line to the word that means almost the same thing.

   jump •   • munch

   eat •   • sniff

   smell •   • hop

 Convention   Trace over the question mark.

An asking sentence
ends with a question
mark.

What do you smell?

 **Word Choice**   Use good action words.

A. Look at each picture.
How does the person or animal move?
Write the action word on the line.

1. bunny _____

2. birds _____

3. fish _____

4. girl _____

B. What is your favorite action word?

_____

 Convention

An asking sentence ends with a question mark.

Finish the sentence.
Write a question mark.

What do you like to play_____

DAY 1

Read the rule aloud. Then guide students through the activities. For example:

- Have students repeat after you as you read each word in the box. Say: *These are all describing words that tell what something looks like. Let's choose the right word for each picture.*

- Call students' attention to item 1. Ask: *What are these? What is the boy wearing?* (pants) Then say: *We can tell more about the pants. We can describe them. Look how the pants don't go all the way down to the boy's shoes. Which word in the box tells about the pants? Which word describes how they look?* (**short**) Say: *The pants are too short.* Have students trace over the word. Repeat the process for items 2–5.

Convention: Read the rule. Say: *A store is one kind of special place. When you're writing the name of a store, begin each word with a capital letter.* Then read each store name aloud as students circle its capital letters.

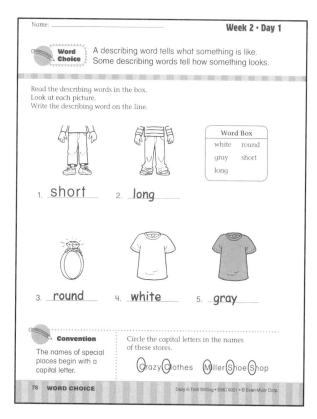

DAY 2

Read the rule aloud. Then guide students through the activities. For example:

- **Activity A:** Read item 1 aloud. Then ask: *Which picture shows a dish that smells stinky? How do you know?* (the bottom one; it looks dirty) Have students draw a line from the sentence to the picture. Repeat for item 2.

- **Activity B:** Read aloud the words in the word box and have students repeat them. Then direct students' attention to the cookie box. Read the label aloud. Ask: *Which word tells how cookies taste?* (**sweet**) Have students trace over the word. Repeat for the remaining pictures.

Convention: Review the rule. Remind students that each word in the name of a store is capitalized. Read the store name aloud, and have students trace over the capital letters.

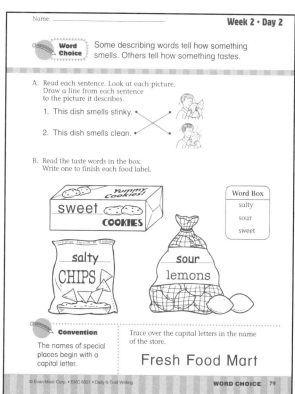

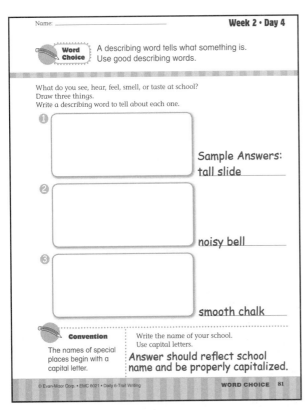

DAY 3

Read the rule aloud. Then guide students through the activities. For example:

- Read aloud the words in the box and have students repeat them.

- Read item 1 aloud. Point out the grill in the picture and ask: *Which word describes how the fire feels?* (**hot**) Have students trace over the word. Repeat the process for items 2–6, but have students write the word from the box on the line.

Convention: Read the rule. Say: *Names of places, such as parks or libraries, also need capital letters.* Guide students to write the name of the park with capital letters.

DAY 4

Read the rule aloud. Say: *A good describing word tells exactly what something is like.* Then guide students through the activities. For example:

- Brainstorm places or objects at the school that can be described. (e.g., library, pencil) List possibilities and invite students to give describing words for each one. Remind students: *You can use many different describing words to tell about the same thing.*

- As a class, choose three things. Have students draw a picture of each. Then have them choose the best word to describe each thing. Have students write the words next to the pictures.

Convention: Read the rule aloud. Say: *Names of schools also need capital letters.* Write your school's name on the board for students to copy.

DAY 5 *Writing Prompt*

- Form a sentence about one of the places or objects described on Day 4. For example: (*School name*) *has a tall slide.* Have students copy the sentence. Then have them write a sentence of their own, using a different describing word.

- Remind students to capitalize the school name.

Name: _____

 **Word Choice**

A describing word tells what something is like.
Some describing words tell how something looks.

Read the describing words in the box.
Look at each picture.
Write the describing word on the line.

Word Box	
white	round
gray	short
long	

1. short

2. _____

3. _____   4. _____   5. _____

 Convention

The names of special places begin with a capital letter.

Circle the capital letters in the names of these stores.

Crazy Clothes   Miller Shoe Shop

 **Word Choice**   Some describing words tell how something smells. Others tell how something tastes.

A. Read each sentence. Look at each picture.
Draw a line from each sentence
to the picture it describes.

1. This dish smells stinky. •   •

2. This dish smells clean. •   •

B. Read the taste words in the box.
Write one to finish each food label.

Word Box
salty
sour
sweet

sweet

 Convention

The names of special places begin with a capital letter.

Trace over the capital letters in the name of the store.

Fresh Food Mart

 **Word Choice** Some describing words tell how something sounds. Others tell how something feels.

Read the words in the word box.
Use the words to complete the sentences.

1. The fire is ___hot___.

2. The ice cream is _____.

3. The radio is _____.

4. The dog sleeps on the _____ grass.

Word Box	
cold	loud
hard	quiet
hot	soft

5. The dog is _____.

6. The sidewalk is _____.

 **Convention**

The names of special places begin with a capital letter.

Copy the name of the park.
Use capital letters.

center park _____

Word Choice A describing word tells what something is.
Use good describing words.

What do you see, hear, feel, smell, or taste at school?
Draw three things.
Write a describing word to tell about each one.

1

_____

2

_____

3

_____

Convention

The names of special places begin with a capital letter.

Write the name of your school.
Use capital letters.

_____

WORD CHOICE
Use Words to Tell How You Feel

DAY 1

Read the rule aloud. Say: *When you write, one way to tell about yourself or someone else is to tell about feelings. This week, we'll learn feeling words and practice using them.* Then guide students through the activities. For example:

- Read the title and direct students through the story. For the first picture, say: *This is Elena. She has a brownie in her hand. Look at her face. How do you think she feels?* (happy) Point out the plate with two brownies on it.

- Continue to direct students through the story, explaining that a plate of brownies is being passed around. By the time the plate reaches James and Mary, there are no brownies left.

- Read aloud the words in the word box and have students repeat them. Then read item 1 aloud. Point out Elena's expression and ask: *Which word tells how she feels?* (**happy**) Have students trace the word on the line. Repeat the process for items 2–5, but have students write the word from the box on the line.

Convention: Read the rule aloud. Say: *Sometimes you have a really strong feeling, like James did in the story. We use an exclamation point to show that a feeling is strong.* Read the sample sentence. Ask: *Can you find the exclamation point at the end of the sentence?* Have students point to it and circle it.

DAY 2

Read the rule aloud. Say: *Today, we will learn more feeling words.* Then guide students through the activity. For example:

- For item 1, say: **Hungry** *is a feeling.* Ask: *What does* **hungry** *mean?* (You want food.) Have students trace over the word and say it aloud. Repeat the process for each word.

- Return to item 1 and say: *Let's find the picture of the boy who is hungry.* Point out the picture of the boy taking the sandwich. Say: *He looks happy to be taking the sandwich. He is probably hungry.* Have students draw a line from the word to the picture. Repeat the process for each item.

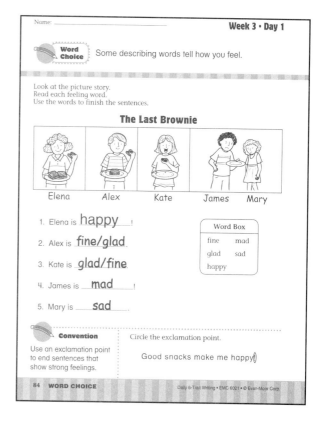

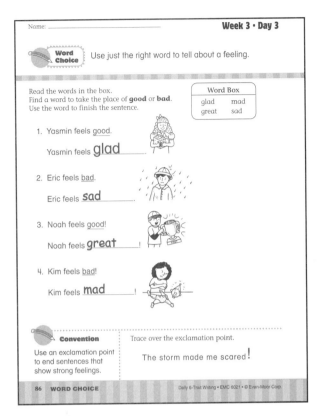

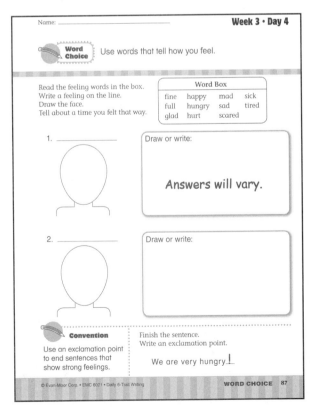

DAY 3

Read the rule aloud. Then guide students through the activities. For example:

- Read aloud each word in the word box and have students repeat them. Then read the first sentence in item 1 aloud. Say: *We often use the word* **good** *to tell how we feel. But* **good** *can mean many things. You can feel happy, great, glad, cheerful, or excited.*

- Point to the picture and ask: *Which word tells exactly how Yasmin feels?* (**glad**) Say: **Glad** *is a better word. Let's change the sentence.* Have students trace over **glad** in the second sentence and read the new sentence aloud. Repeat for items 2–4.

Convention: Review the rule. Read the sentence aloud before students complete the activity.

DAY 4

Review the rule. Then guide students through the activities. For example:

- Read aloud each word in the box. Then model item 1. For example: Write **hurt**. Say: *When I'm* **hurt**, *I frown. I also cry.* Draw a face on the board with a frown and tears. Then say: *Now I'll think of a time when I was hurt. Once when I was ice-skating, I hurt my knee.* Draw a relevant picture, such as a stick figure on skates, and write a word to tell about it, such as **knee** or **skate**.

- Complete the page as a class, choosing a feeling word and having students think of individual experiences to draw and write about.

Convention: Review the rule. Read the sentence aloud before students complete the activity.

DAY 5 *Writing Prompt*

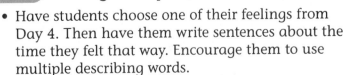

- Have students choose one of their feelings from Day 4. Then have them write sentences about the time they felt that way. Encourage them to use multiple describing words.

- Remind students to use exclamation points.

Name: _____

 **Word Choice**   Some describing words tell how you feel.

Look at the picture story.
Read each feeling word.
Use the words to finish the sentences.

The Last Brownie

Elena   Alex   Kate   James   Mary

1. Elena is ___happy___!

2. Alex is _____.

3. Kate is _____.

4. James is _____!

5. Mary is _____.

Word Box	
fine	mad
glad	sad
happy	

Convention

Use an exclamation point
to end sentences that
show strong feelings.

Circle the exclamation point.

Good snacks make me happy!

 **Word Choice** Use words that tell how you feel.

Trace over each feeling word.
Draw a line to the picture that shows the feeling.

1. <u>hungry</u> •

2. <u>full</u> •

3. <u>hurt</u> •

4. <u>sick</u> •

5. <u>scared</u> •

6. <u>tired</u> •

Name: _____

Word Choice   Use just the right word to tell about a feeling.

Read the words in the box.
Find a word to take the place of **good** or **bad**.
Use the word to finish the sentence.

Word Box	
glad	mad
great	sad

1. Yasmin feels <u>good</u>.

   Yasmin feels glad_____.

2. Eric feels <u>bad</u>.

   Eric feels _____.

3. Noah feels <u>good</u>!

   Noah feels _____!

4. Kim feels <u>bad</u>!

   Kim feels _____!

Convention

Use an exclamation point
to end sentences that
show strong feelings.

Trace over the exclamation point.

The storm made me scared!

Name: _____

 **Word Choice** Use words that tell how you feel.

Read the feeling words in the box.
Write a feeling on the line.
Draw the face.
Tell about a time you felt that way.

Word Box			
fine	happy	mad	sick
full	hungry	sad	tired
glad	hurt	scared	

1. _____

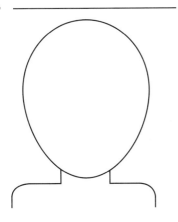

Draw or write:

2. _____

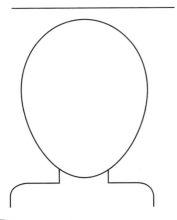

Draw or write:

 Convention

Use an exclamation point to end sentences that show strong feelings.

Finish the sentence.
Write an exclamation point.

We are very hungry___

DAY 1

Read the rule aloud. Say: *A naming word tells about a person, place, or thing. We will learn how to use good naming words today.* Then guide students through the activities. For example:

- Have students point to each picture and repeat after you as you read the label aloud. Then read aloud the first sentence in item 1. Say: *Boy is a naming word. But we don't know who the boy is.* Point out the picture of Cory. Say: *Cory is a better word, because it tells exactly who the sentence is about. Let's change the sentence.* Have students trace over the word. Then read aloud the new sentence. Repeat the process for items 2–4.

- To summarize the point of the activity, have students listen as you reread the first sentence in each item: *The boy wakes up. He eats food for breakfast.*, etc. Then reread the second sentence in each item: *Cory wakes up. He eats rice for breakfast.*, etc. Then ask: *Which story sounded better—the first or the second?* Explain that good writers use specific naming words.

Convention: Read the rule aloud. Then say: *Some people have special words in front of their last names, such as **Mr.**, **Mrs.**, **Ms.**, or **Dr.** Always start these words with a capital letter.* Have students point to each capital letter in the activity before they circle it.

DAY 2

Read the rule aloud and review what a describing word is. (It tells what something is like.) Then guide students through the activities. For example:

- Read aloud the two words for item 1. Say: *Big and huge have almost the same meaning.*

- Direct students' attention to the pictures. Say: *This gorilla is big. But the elephant is really, really big! Huge is another word for **really, really big**. So, the gorilla is **big**, but the elephant is **huge**.* Have students trace and write the words. Repeat the process for items 2–4.

Convention: Review the rule. Point out how **Mr.** and **Ms.** end with a period. Then have students trace over the titles.

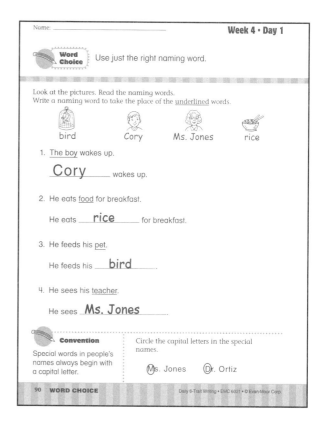

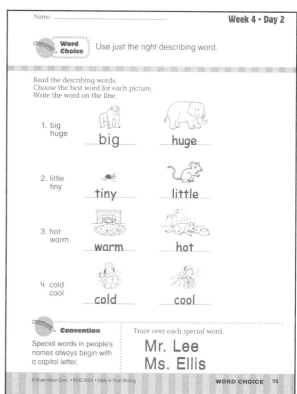

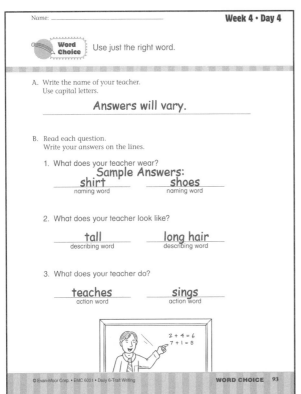

DAY 3

Read the rule aloud and review what an action word is. (It tells what people or things do.) Then guide students through the activities. For example:

- Say: ***Says** is an action word. But there are many ways you can **say** something.* Then point to the word box and say: *These are some words you can use instead of **says**.* Explain the meaning of each word: ***Asks** is when you say a question. **Calls** is when you say someone's name to get his or her attention. **Tells** is when you say something in a normal voice. **Yells** is when you say something in a loud voice.*

- Point out the first cartoon panel. Read aloud the speech balloon and say: *Dad wants to find Rosa. He **calls** her.* Have students trace over the word. Repeat the process for the other panels.

Convention: Review the rule. Remind students that both words need to start with capital letters.

DAY 4

Read the rule aloud. Say: *Today, we will use all kinds of words to tell about someone we know.* Then guide students through the activities. For example:

- **Activity A:** Write your name on the board for students to copy.

- **Activity B:** Read aloud each question, inviting students to brainstorm answers. Encourage students to think of specific, "just the right" words that tell about the subject. On the board, list possibilities for each question. Have students select words or phrases to copy onto their papers.

DAY 5 · *Writing Prompt*

- Use the brainstormed words from Day 4 to form one or two sentences about yourself. Have students copy the sentences and write at least one of their own. Students may also want to draw a picture to illustrate their sentences.

- Remind students to capitalize your title and name.

Name: _____

 **Word Choice** Use just the right naming word.

Look at the pictures. Read the naming words.
Write a naming word to take the place of the <u>underlined</u> words.

bird

Cory

Ms. Jones

rice

1. <u>The boy</u> wakes up.

   _Cory_____ wakes up.

2. He eats <u>food</u> for breakfast.

   He eats _____ for breakfast.

3. He feeds his <u>pet</u>.

   He feeds his _____.

4. He sees his <u>teacher</u>.

   He sees _____.

 Convention

Special words in people's names always begin with a capital letter.

Circle the capital letters in the special names.

Ms. Jones   Dr. Ortiz

 **Word Choice**   Use just the right describing word.

Read the describing words.
Choose the best word for each picture.
Write the word on the line.

1. big
   huge

   _____big_____   _____

2. little
   tiny

   _____   _____

3. hot
   warm

   _____   _____

4. cold
   cool

   _____   _____

 Convention   Trace over each special word.

Special words in people's
names always begin with
a capital letter.

Mr. Lee
Ms. Ellis

 **Word Choice**   Use just the right action word.

Read the story about Rosa and Dad. Use the words from the word box to complete the sentences.

| **Words for "Says"** |
| asks   calls   tells   yells |

Dad __calls__ Rosa.

Rosa _____ to Dad.

Dad _____ Rosa.

Rosa _____ Dad.

Convention

Special words in people's names always begin with a capital letter.

Rewrite this name.
Use capital letters.

dr. chan _____

Word Choice   Use just the right word.

A. Write the name of your teacher.
   Use capital letters.

   _____

B. Read each question.
   Write your answers on the lines.

   1. What does your teacher wear?

      _____   _____
      naming word   naming word

   2. What does your teacher look like?

      _____   _____
      describing word   describing word

   3. What does your teacher do?

      _____   _____
      action word   action word

DAY 1

Read the rule aloud. Then guide students through the activities. For example:

- Read aloud each word in the word box and have students repeat after you. Then read aloud the sentence in item 1. Point to the picture and ask: *Is the sentence correct? Are the foxes eating?* (No; they are climbing.)

- Say: *The action word is not correct! Let's change it.* Have students trace over the line on **eat** and trace over **climb** on the line. Repeat this process for items 2–4, explaining that if the action word matches the picture, students do not need to change the sentence.

Convention: Read the rule and directions aloud. Then point to the first word in the activity. Say: *Foxes is a naming word. It tells about more than one fox, so there is an es at the end.* Model pronouncing the word, emphasizing that the word has two syllables now. Have students repeat the word before circling the **es**. Repeat the process for the next word.

DAY 2

Read the rule aloud. Then guide students through the activities. For example:

- Say: *Today, we'll read sentences and fill in two types of words: describing words and naming words.* If necessary, remind students of the difference between the two. Read aloud the words in each box and have students repeat after you.

- Read item 1 aloud: *The ___ is tiny.* Then point to the picture and explain that it shows four toys of different sizes. Say: *We are looking for something tiny.* Ask: *What does tiny mean?* (very little) *Which toy is tiny?* (the truck) Have students trace over the word and read the completed sentence aloud. Repeat this process for items 2–4.

Convention: Read the rule and directions aloud. Point out each word and read it aloud as students fill in the **es**. Then read the plural noun aloud and have students repeat after you.

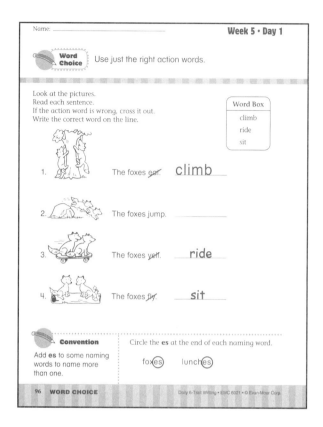

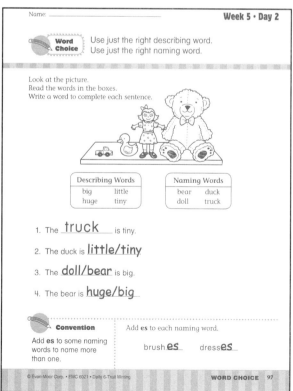

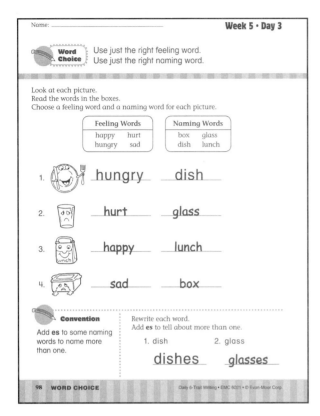

Name: _____   **Week 5 • Day 3**

Word Choice
Use just the right feeling word.
Use just the right naming word.

Look at each picture.
Read the words in the boxes.
Choose a feeling word and a naming word for each picture.

Feeling Words	
happy	hurt
hungry	sad

Naming Words	
box	glass
dish	lunch

1. hungry   dish

2. hurt   glass

3. happy   lunch

4. sad   box

Convention
Add **es** to some naming words to name more than one.

Rewrite each word.
Add **es** to tell about more than one.

1. dish   2. glass

dishes   glasses

98 WORD CHOICE   Daily 6-Trait Writing • EMC 6021 • © Evan-Moor Corp.

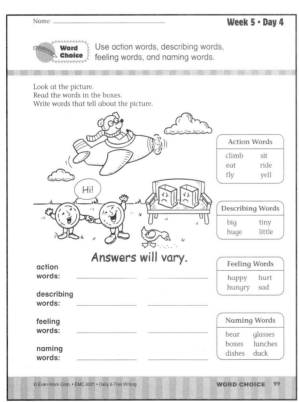

Name: _____   **Week 5 • Day 4**

Word Choice
Use action words, describing words, feeling words, and naming words.

Look at the picture.
Read the words in the boxes.
Write words that tell about the picture.

Hi!

Answers will vary.

Action Words	
climb	sit
eat	ride
fly	yell

Describing Words	
big	tiny
huge	little

Feeling Words	
happy	hurt
hungry	sad

Naming Words	
bear	glasses
boxes	lunches
dishes	duck

action
words: _____

describing
words: _____

feeling
words: _____

naming
words: _____

© Evan-Moor Corp. • EMC 6021 • Daily 6-Trait Writing   **WORD CHOICE 99**

DAY 3

Read the rule aloud. Then guide students through the activities. For example:

- Say: *Today, we'll look at pictures and fill in two types of words: feeling words and naming words.* Read aloud the words in each box and have students repeat after you.

- Point out the picture in item 1. Ask: *What feeling word do you see?* (**hungry**) Have students trace over the word. Then ask: *Which naming word matches the picture?* (**dish**) Have students trace over the word on the second line. Then have students read aloud the phrase. (**hungry dish**) Repeat these steps for items 2–4.

Convention: Review the rule. Read the first word aloud. Say: *We add **es** to **dish** to tell about more than one.* Have students write the word, and repeat for **glass**.

DAY 4

Read the rule aloud. Then guide students through the activity. For example:

- Point out the picture. Say: *We'll write words that tell what is in this picture.* Then point out the word **boxes**. Say: *These are words to choose from. But not all of the words tell about the picture. We have to choose only the ones that tell about the picture.*

- Read aloud each word in the "Action Words" box. (You may want to skip this if students can read them independently.) Then ask: *Which actions are happening in the picture?* (eat, fly, etc.) Have students choose and write one or two words on the lines. Repeat this for each word box.

DAY 5 *Writing Prompt*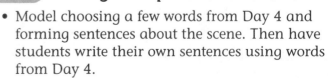

- Model choosing a few words from Day 4 and forming sentences about the scene. Then have students write their own sentences using words from Day 4.

- Remind students to correctly spell plural nouns that end with **es**.

Name: _____

 **Word Choice**   Use just the right action words.

Look at the pictures.
Read each sentence.
If the action word is wrong, cross it out.
Write the correct word on the line.

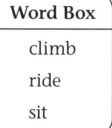

Word Box
climb
ride
sit

1.   The foxes ~~eat.~~   climb _____

2.   The foxes jump.   _____

3.   The foxes yell.   _____

4.   The foxes fly.   _____

 Convention

Add **es** to some naming words to name more than one.

Circle the **es** at the end of each naming word.

foxes   lunches

Word Choice

Use just the right describing word.
Use just the right naming word.

Look at the picture.
Read the words in the boxes.
Write a word to complete each sentence.

Describing Words	
big	little
huge	tiny

Naming Words	
bear	duck
doll	truck

1. The ___truck___ is tiny.

2. The duck is _____.

3. The _____ is big.

4. The bear is _____.

Convention

Add **es** to some naming words to name more than one.

Add **es** to each naming word.

brush_____   dress_____

 **Word Choice**   Use just the right feeling word.
Use just the right naming word.

Look at each picture.
Read the words in the boxes.
Choose a feeling word and a naming word for each picture.

Feeling Words		Naming Words	
happy	hurt	box	glass
hungry	sad	dish	lunch

1. _hungry_ _dish_

2. _____ _____

3. _____ _____

4. _____ _____

Convention

Add **es** to some naming
words to name more
than one.

Rewrite each word.
Add **es** to tell about more than one.

1. dish   2. glass

dishes   _____

Name: _____

Word Choice Use action words, describing words, feeling words, and naming words.

Look at the picture.
Read the words in the boxes.
Write words that tell about the picture.

Action Words	
climb	sit
eat	ride
fly	yell

Describing Words	
big	tiny
huge	little

Feeling Words	
happy	hurt
hungry	sad

Naming Words	
bear	glasses
boxes	lunches
dishes	duck

action words: _____ _____

describing words: _____ _____

feeling words: _____ _____

naming words: _____ _____

SENTENCE FLUENCY
Write a Sentence

Refer to pages 6 and 7 to introduce or review the writing trait.

DAY 1

Briefly review what students might know about a sentence. (e.g., It starts with a capital letter. It ends with an end mark.) Then read the rule aloud and guide students through the activities. For example:

- **Activity A:** Read aloud each sentence for item 1. Say: *The first sentence tells about walking to school. But, we don't know who is walking to school! It is not a complete sentence. The second sentence tells us it is Katy who walks to school. This is the complete sentence.* Have students circle the sentence. Repeat the process for item 2.

- **Activity B:** Read aloud the words and phrases in the word box. Then read aloud item 1. Ask: *Which word or words make this a complete sentence?* (**The girl**) Have students trace over the phrase and read the completed sentence aloud. Repeat the process for items 2–4, but have students write the word or words on the line.

Convention: Read the rule and each item aloud. Say: *Both of these words need an s to tell about more than one.* Have students complete the activity.

DAY 2

Read the rule aloud. Then guide students through the activities. For example:

- **Activity A:** Read aloud item 1. Then repeat the phrase with each answer choice. (e.g., *"The kite are in the water,"* etc.) Ask: *Which one makes a complete sentence that also makes sense?* (**The kite flies in the sky.**) Have students connect the correct phrases. Repeat the process for items 2–4.

- **Activity B:** Read aloud the words in item 1. Ask: *In which order should we write the words to make a sentence?* Try out a few possibilities, such as *fish swims The* or *The swims fish.* Have students choose the correct order for writing a sentence, reminding them to start with a capital letter and end with a period. Repeat the process for item 2.

Convention: Read the rule and each item aloud. Say: *Both of these words need es to tell about more than one.* Have students complete the activity.

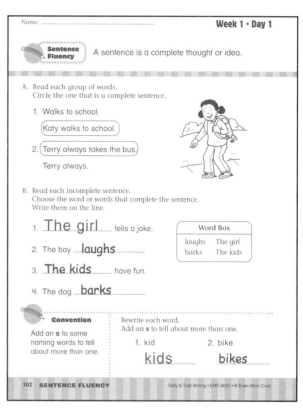

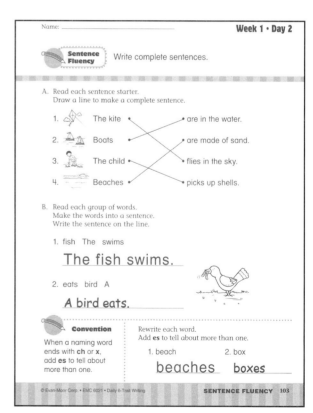

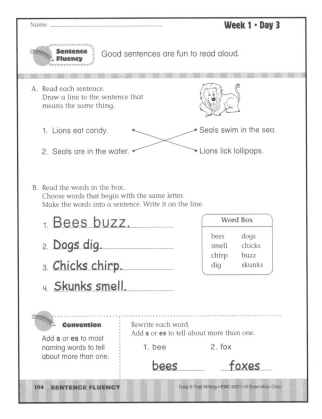

DAY 3

Read the rule aloud. Then guide students through the activities. For example:

- **Activity A:** Read aloud item 1. Read aloud both answer choices and ask: *Which sentence means the same as item 1?* (**Lions lick lollipops.**) Have students draw a line to connect the two. Explain that both sentences mean the same thing, but the second has a more fun sound because all of the words start with the same letter. Repeat the process for item 2.

- **Activity B:** Say: *We can make our own sentences that are fun to read aloud.* Read the words in the box. Model forming a sentence for item 1. Say: *Let's write a sentence about bees. Which word tells what bees do?* (**buzz**) *Here is my sentence: "Bees buzz."* Have students trace over the sentence. Repeat the process for items 2–4.

Convention: Review the rule. Read each item aloud. You may want to model using a children's dictionary to find the correct plural spelling for each word. Then have students complete the activity.

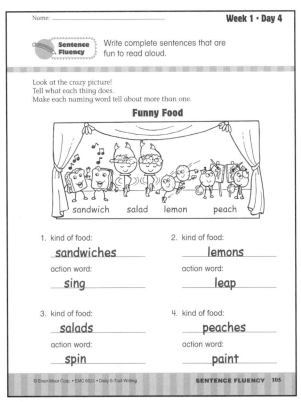

DAY 4

Read the rule aloud. Then guide students through the activity. For example:

- Say: *Let's write what these funny foods are doing!* Point out each food in the picture and its corresponding naming word. Then point out item 1. Say: *Write the word* **sandwich** *to tell the kind of food.* Then say: *There is more than one sandwich in the picture. What do we add to the word* **sandwich** *to tell about more than one?* (**es**)

- Have students give action words that go with each food. Guide students to name action words that start with the same sounds as the naming words to make them fun to read aloud.

DAY 5 *Writing Prompt*

- Have students write sentences about the picture in Day 4. They should use the words they wrote to describe the picture.

- Remind students to spell plural nouns correctly.

 **Sentence Fluency**   A sentence is a complete thought or idea.

A. Read each group of words.
   Circle the one that is a complete sentence.

   1. Walks to school.

      Katy walks to school.

   2. Terry always takes the bus.

      Terry always.

B. Read each incomplete sentence.
   Choose the word or words that complete the sentence.
   Write them on the line.

   1. <u>The girl</u> tells a joke.

   2. The boy _____.

   3. _____ have fun.

   4. The dog _____.

Word Box	
laughs	The girl
barks	The kids

 Convention

Add an **s** to some naming words to tell about more than one.

Rewrite each word.
Add an **s** to tell about more than one.

1. kid   2. bike

   <u>kids</u>   _____

 **Sentence Fluency**   Write complete sentences.

A. Read each sentence starter.
   Draw a line to make a complete sentence.

   1. ![kite] The kite •   • are in the water.

   2. ![boats] Boats •   • are made of sand.

   3. ![child] The child •   • flies in the sky.

   4. ![beaches] Beaches •   • picks up shells.

B. Read each group of words.
   Make the words into a sentence.
   Write the sentence on the line.

   1. fish   The   swims

      The fish swims.

   2. eats   bird   A

      _____

 Convention   Rewrite each word.
                        Add **es** to tell about more than one.

When a naming word
ends with **ch** or **x**,   1. beach   2. box
add **es** to tell about
more than one.   beaches   _____

Name: _____

 **Sentence Fluency** — Good sentences are fun to read aloud.

A. Read each sentence.
Draw a line to the sentence that means the same thing.

1. Lions eat candy. •   • Seals swim in the sea.

2. Seals are in the water. •   • Lions lick lollipops.

B. Read the words in the box.
Choose words that begin with the same letter.
Make the words into a sentence. Write it on the line.

1. Bees buzz. _____

2. _____

3. _____

4. _____

Word Box	
bees	dogs
smell	chicks
chirp	buzz
dig	skunks

 Convention

Add **s** or **es** to most naming words to tell about more than one.

Rewrite each word.
Add **s** or **es** to tell about more than one.

1. bee   2. fox

_____   _____

        Daily 6-Trait Writing • EMC 6021 • © Evan-Moor Corp.

Sentence Fluency

Write complete sentences that are
fun to read aloud.

Look at the crazy picture!
Tell what each thing does.
Make each naming word tell about more than one.

Funny Food

sandwich   salad   lemon   peach

1. kind of food:

_____

action word:

_____

2. kind of food:

_____

action word:

_____

3. kind of food:

_____

action word:

_____

4. kind of food:

_____

action word:

_____

DAY 1

Read the rule aloud. Then guide students through the activities. For example:

- **Activity A:** Read aloud each word in the box and have students repeat them. Then read aloud item 1. Ask: *What is the naming word?* (**Becky**) Say: *In a sentence, the describing word can come after the naming word.* Point to the picture and ask: *Which word tells how Becky feels?* (**glad**) Have students trace over the word. Point out the word in between the naming and describing words. (**feels**) Repeat the process for items 2–4.

- **Activity B:** Read the words aloud. Say: *In our new sentence, let's put the describing word after the naming word. How will the sentence sound?* Try possible combinations, such as "The hot dogs yummy are," until students identify the correct order. Have them write the sentence on the line.

Convention: Read the rule aloud. Then point out the water bottle in the picture. Say: *The water belongs to Becky. Let's write an apostrophe and s after the word* **Becky.**

DAY 2

Read the rule aloud. Then guide students through the activities. For example:

- **Activity A:** Read aloud each word in the box and have students repeat them. Point out the picture. Then read aloud item 1. Ask: *Which word tells how the kids feel?* (**happy**) Say: *Let's add the word to the sentence. This time, we'll put it before the naming word it describes.* Have students trace over the word. Repeat the process for items 2–4.

- **Activity B:** Read the words aloud. Ask: *Which one is the describing word?* (**tired**) *Which one is the naming word?* (**boys**) Say: *We will write a sentence with* **tired boys** *in it.* If necessary, help students determine the word order. Then have them write the sentence on the line.

Convention: Review the rule. Then read the activity words aloud. Say: *We are telling about the mother of Mike. We say* **Mike's mother.** *Where should we put the apostrophe and s?* (after **Mike**) Have students complete the activity.

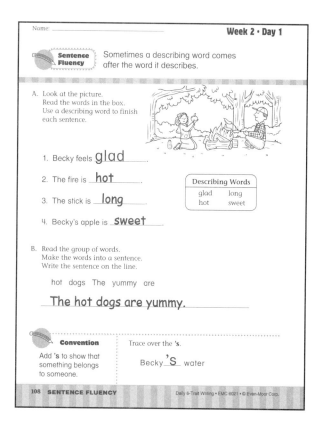

Name: _____   Week 2 • Day 1

Sentence Fluency — Sometimes a describing word comes after the word it describes.

A. Look at the picture.
   Read the words in the box.
   Use a describing word to finish each sentence.

1. Becky feels glad
2. The fire is hot
3. The stick is long
4. Becky's apple is sweet

Describing Words
glad   long
hot   sweet

B. Read the group of words.
   Make the words into a sentence.
   Write the sentence on the line.

hot dogs The yummy are

The hot dogs are yummy.

Convention
Add **'s** to show that something belongs to someone.

Trace over the **'s**.

Becky**'s** water

108 SENTENCE FLUENCY   Daily 6-Trait Writing • EMC 6021 • © Evan-Moor Corp.

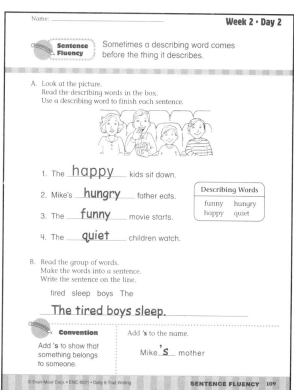

Name: _____   Week 2 • Day 2

Sentence Fluency — Sometimes a describing word comes before the thing it describes.

A. Look at the picture.
   Read the describing words in the box.
   Use a describing word to finish each sentence.

1. The happy kids sit down.
2. Mike's hungry father eats.
3. The funny movie starts.
4. The quiet children watch.

Describing Words
funny   hungry
happy   quiet

B. Read the group of words.
   Make the words into a sentence.
   Write the sentence on the line.

tired sleep boys The

The tired boys sleep.

Convention
Add **'s** to show that something belongs to someone.

Add **'s** to the name.

Mike**'s** mother

© Evan-Moor Corp. • EMC 6021 • Daily 6-Trait Writing   SENTENCE FLUENCY 109

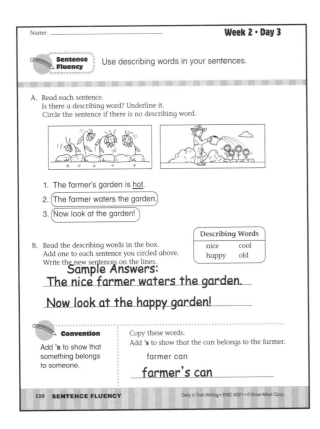

Name: _____

Sentence Fluency Use describing words in your sentences.

A. Read each sentence.
Is there a describing word? Underline it.
Circle the sentence if there is no describing word.

1. The farmer's garden is <u>hot</u>.
2. The farmer waters the garden.
3. Now look at the garden!

Describing Words

| nice | cool |
| happy | old |

B. Read the describing words in the box.
Add one to each sentence you circled above.
Write the new sentences on the lines.

Sample Answers:
The nice farmer waters the garden.

Now look at the happy garden!

Convention
Add **'s** to show that something belongs to someone.

Copy these words.
Add **'s** to show that the can belongs to the farmer.

farmer can

farmer's can

110 SENTENCE FLUENCY   Daily 6-Trait Writing • EMC 6021 • © Evan-Moor Corp.

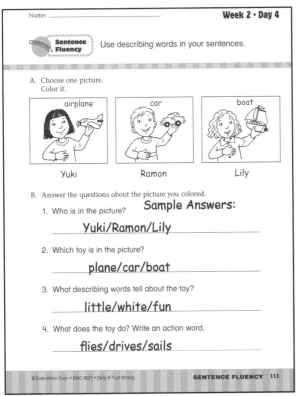

Name: _____

Sentence Fluency Use describing words in your sentences.

A. Choose one picture.
Color it.

airplane   car   boat

Yuki   Ramon   Lily

B. Answer the questions about the picture you colored.
Sample Answers:

1. Who is in the picture?
   Yuki/Ramon/Lily

2. Which toy is in the picture?
   plane/car/boat

3. What describing words tell about the toy?
   little/white/fun

4. What does the toy do? Write an action word.
   flies/drives/sails

© Evan-Moor Corp. • EMC 6021 • Daily 6-Trait Writing   SENTENCE FLUENCY 111

DAY 3

Read the rule aloud. Then guide students through the activities. For example:

- **Activity A:** Have students describe the pictures. Then read item 1 aloud. Ask: *Is there a describing word in this sentence?* (yes) *What is it?* (**hot**) Have students underline it. Then read aloud item 2. Ask: *Is there a describing word?* (no) Have students circle the sentence. Repeat for item 3.

- **Activity B:** Read aloud each word in the box and have students repeat them. Then return to item 2 in Activity A. Say: *We circled this sentence because it has no describing word. Which words from the box could we add?* (**nice, happy, old**) Model choosing one word, such as **nice**. Ask: *What would our new sentence be?* (The nice farmer waters the garden.) Have students choose a word and write their new sentence on the first line. Repeat with item 3.

Convention: Read the rule aloud. Say: *The watering can belongs to the farmer. What do we do to the word farmer?* (add an apostrophe and **s**) Have students write the phrase.

DAY 4

Read the rule aloud. Then guide students through the activities. For example:

- **Activity A:** Point out the first picture. Say: *This is Yuki. What does Yuki have?* (an airplane) Repeat the process for the next two pictures. Then have students choose one picture and color it.

- **Activity B:** Read aloud question 1 and model finding a name. Then guide students through questions 2–4, eliciting possible answers. Write students' suggestions on the board for them to copy.

DAY 5 *Writing Prompt*

- Have students write two sentences using their answers from Day 4. For example: *Yuki's plane is blue. The little plane flies.*

- Remind students to spell possessive nouns correctly.

Sentence
Fluency

Sometimes a describing word comes
after the word it describes.

A. Look at the picture.
Read the words in the box.
Use a describing word to finish
each sentence.

1. Becky feels _glad_____.

2. The fire is _____.

3. The stick is _____.

4. Becky's apple is _____.

Describing Words	
glad	long
hot	sweet

B. Read the group of words.
Make the words into a sentence.
Write the sentence on the line.

    hot dogs The yummy are

_____

Convention

Add **'s** to show that
something belongs
to someone.

Trace over the **'s**.

Becky_'s_ water

 **Sentence Fluency**   Sometimes a describing word comes before the thing it describes.

A. Look at the picture.
    Read the describing words in the box.
    Use a describing word to finish each sentence.

1. The ___happy___ kids sit down.

2. Mike's _____ father eats.

3. The _____ movie starts.

4. The _____ children watch.

Describing Words	
funny	hungry
happy	quiet

B. Read the group of words.
    Make the words into a sentence.
    Write the sentence on the line.

    tired   sleep   boys   The

    _____

Convention

Add **'s** to show that something belongs to someone.

Add **'s** to the name.

Mike_____ mother

 **Sentence Fluency**   Use describing words in your sentences.

A. Read each sentence.
    Is there a describing word? Underline it.
    Circle the sentence if there is no describing word.

1. The farmer's garden is hot.

2. The farmer waters the garden.

3. Now look at the garden!

B. Read the describing words in the box.
    Add one to each sentence you circled above.
    Write the new sentences on the lines.

Describing Words	
nice	cool
happy	old

_____

_____

 Convention

Add **'s** to show that something belongs to someone.

Copy these words.
Add **'s** to show that the can belongs to the farmer.

farmer can

_____

Sentence Fluency   Use describing words in your sentences.

A. Choose one picture.
    Color it.

Yuki

Ramon

Lily

B. Answer the questions about the picture you colored.

   1. Who is in the picture?

   _____

   2. Which toy is in the picture?

   _____

   3. What describing words tell about the toy?

   _____

   4. What does the toy do? Write an action word.

   _____

SENTENCE FLUENCY
Write Longer Sentences

DAY 1

Read the rule aloud. Say: *This week, we'll learn how to make longer sentences. One way to do this is to tell **how** something happens.* Then guide students through the activities. For example:

- **Activity A:** Read aloud the words in the box and have students repeat them after you. Then read sentence 1. Ask: *Which word tells **how** the lion roars?* (**loudly**) Have students write the word on the line. Repeat the process for sentences 2 and 3.

- **Activity B:** Read item 1 aloud. Then ask: *What is the naming word?* (**snail**) *What is the action word?* (**goes**) *Which word tells **how** the snail goes?* (**slowly**) Then model writing the sentence. (**The snail goes slowly.**) For item 2, repeat the modeling if necessary.

Convention: Read the rule aloud. Then read aloud the activity sentence. Say: *The sentence names three types of animals that are pets. When you tell about three things in a row, separate them with commas. Before the last thing, write a comma and the word **and**.* Then have students trace over the commas.

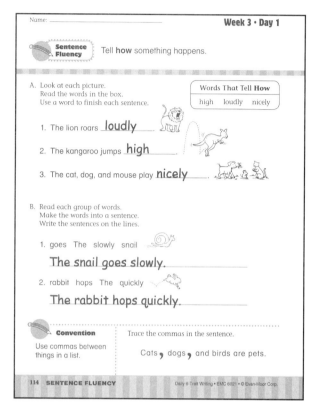

DAY 2

Read the rule aloud. Then guide students through the activities. For example:

- **Activity A:** Read aloud the words and phrases in the box and have students repeat after you. Then read aloud sentence 1. Say: *Look at the picture.* Ask: *Where do the robots eat, sleep, and fly?* (**in the ship**) Have students trace over the answer. Repeat the process for sentences 2 and 3, but have students write the phrase on the line.

- **Activity B:** Read aloud item 1. Prompt students to identify the naming and action words as well as the words that tell **where** and **when**. Then read aloud the words in different combinations until students identify the one that sounds correct. (**Soon the robots stop.**) Have students write the sentence on the line. Repeat for item 2.

Convention: Review the rule. Then read aloud the sentence before having students write in the commas.

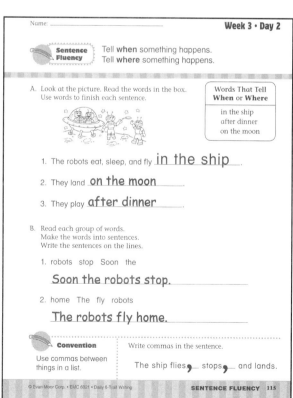

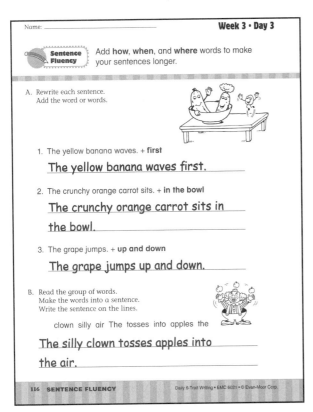

Name: _____   **Week 3 • Day 3**

Sentence Fluency — Add **how**, **when**, and **where** words to make your sentences longer.

A. Rewrite each sentence.
Add the word or words.

1. The yellow banana waves. + **first**

   The yellow banana waves first.

2. The crunchy orange carrot sits. + **in the bowl**

   The crunchy orange carrot sits in
   the bowl.

3. The grape jumps. + **up and down**

   The grape jumps up and down.

B. Read the group of words.
Make the words into a sentence.
Write the sentence on the lines.

   clown silly air The tosses into apples the

   The silly clown tosses apples into
   the air.

116 SENTENCE FLUENCY   Daily 6-Trait Writing • EMC 6021 • © Evan-Moor Corp.

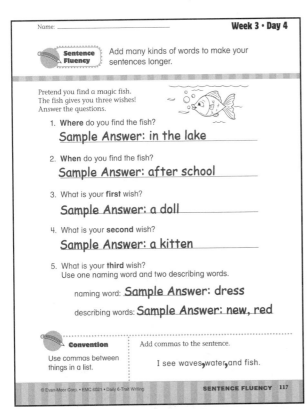

Name: _____   **Week 3 • Day 4**

Sentence Fluency — Add many kinds of words to make your sentences longer.

Pretend you find a magic fish.
The fish gives you three wishes!
Answer the questions.

1. **Where** do you find the fish?
   Sample Answer: in the lake

2. **When** do you find the fish?
   Sample Answer: after school

3. What is your **first** wish?
   Sample Answer: a doll

4. What is your **second** wish?
   Sample Answer: a kitten

5. What is your **third** wish?
   Use one naming word and two describing words.

   naming word: Sample Answer: dress

   describing words: Sample Answer: new, red

Convention
Use commas between things in a list.

   I see waves, water, and fish.

© Evan-Moor Corp. • EMC 6021 • Daily 6-Trait Writing   SENTENCE FLUENCY 117

DAY 3

Read the rule aloud. Then say: *We know how to add words that tell **how**, **when**, and **where** to our sentences. Today, we will practice writing longer sentences.* Then guide students through the activities. For example:

- **Activity A:** Read item 1 aloud. Say: *We can add the word **first** to tell **when**. How would the sentence sound?* (**The yellow banana waves first.**) Write the sentence on the board. Have students copy the sentence. Repeat the process for items 2 and 3.

- **Activity B:** Read aloud the group of words. Prompt students to find the action word. (**tosses**) Ask: *Which naming word tells something that **tosses**?* (**clown**) Have students try the words in different combinations until they identify a correct order. Have students write the sentence on the lines.

DAY 4

Review the rule. Then guide students through the activities. For example:

- Say: *Pretend you found a magic fish that will grant you three wishes.* Read aloud question 1. Ask: *Where could you find the magic fish?* List possibilities as prepositional phrases. (e.g., at the beach) Have students copy one phrase onto their papers. Guide students to answer questions 2–4.

- For item 5, say: *Let's tell more about this wish! Write what you wish for on the naming word line. What are two words that describe what you wish for? Write those on the describing word lines.*

Convention: Review the rule. Read aloud the sentence before having students complete the activity.

DAY 5 *Writing Prompt*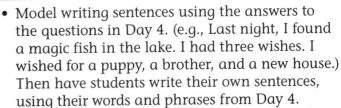

- Model writing sentences using the answers to the questions in Day 4. (e.g., Last night, I found a magic fish in the lake. I had three wishes. I wished for a puppy, a brother, and a new house.) Then have students write their own sentences, using their words and phrases from Day 4.

- Remind students to use commas correctly.

 **Sentence Fluency**

Tell **how** something happens.

A. Look at each picture.
Read the words in the box.
Use a word to finish each sentence.

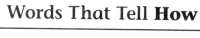

1. The lion roars _____.

2. The kangaroo jumps _____.

3. The cat, dog, and mouse play _____.

B. Read each group of words.
Make the words into a sentence.
Write the sentences on the lines.

1. goes   The   slowly   snail

_____

2. rabbit   hops   The   quickly

_____

 Convention

Use commas between things in a list.

Trace the commas in the sentence.

Cats **,** dogs **,** and birds are pets.

 **Sentence Fluency**

Tell **when** something happens.
Tell **where** something happens.

A. Look at the picture. Read the words in the box.
   Use words to finish each sentence.

Words That Tell **When** or **Where**
in the ship after dinner on the moon

1. The robots eat, sleep, and fly __in the ship__.

2. They land _____.

3. They play _____.

B. Read each group of words.
   Make the words into sentences.
   Write the sentences on the lines.

1. robots   stop   Soon   the

   _____

2. home   The   fly   robots

   _____

 Convention

Use commas between things in a list.

Write commas in the sentence.

The ship flies___ stops___ and lands.

Sentence Fluency

Add **how**, **when**, and **where** words to make your sentences longer.

A. Rewrite each sentence.
   Add the word or words.

1. The yellow banana waves. + **first**

   _____

2. The crunchy orange carrot sits. + **in the bowl**

   _____

   _____

3. The grape jumps. + **up and down**

   _____

B. Read the group of words.
   Make the words into a sentence.
   Write the sentence on the lines.

   clown silly air The tosses into apples the

   _____

   _____

 **Sentence Fluency** Add many kinds of words to make your sentences longer.

Pretend you find a magic fish.
The fish gives you three wishes!
Answer the questions.

1. **Where** do you find the fish?

    _____

2. **When** do you find the fish?

    _____

3. What is your **first** wish?

    _____

4. What is your **second** wish?

    _____

5. What is your **third** wish?
   Use one naming word and two describing words.

   naming word: _____

   describing words: _____   _____

 Convention

Use commas between things in a list.

Add commas to the sentence.

I see waves water and fish.

DAY 1

Read the rule aloud. Then guide students through the activities. For example:

- **Activity A:** Read aloud item 1. Have students find the names (Jada, Erin, and Leah) and underline them. Say: *This writer used the same names over and over again!* Then read aloud item 2 and have students underline the names. For the second sentence, ask: *Is this sentence about Seth?* (yes) Say: *We know it is about Seth because it starts with* **He. He** *means* **Seth**. After reading the third sentence, ask: *Who is* **they**? (Seth, Rick, and Jamie) Say: *Good writers use smaller words such as* **he** *and* **they** *to tell about the same thing.* Then have students circle **he** and **they**.

- **Activity B:** Read aloud the words in the box and have students repeat them. Say: *These are short words that take the place of naming words.* Then read aloud item 1. Ask: *Which word can take the place of* **The bell**? (**It**) Have students write **It** on the line. Repeat for item 2.

Convention: Read the rule aloud. Explain that **can't** is short for **cannot**, which contains the two words **can** and **not**. Then explain that **don't** is short for **do not**. Have students complete the activity.

DAY 2

Read the rule aloud. Then guide students through the activities. For example:

- **Activity A:** Read aloud the naming words in item 1. Point out the next column and ask: *Which word means the same as* **Omar and I**? (**We**) *Draw a line to match the words that mean the same thing.* Repeat for items 2–4.

- **Activity B:** Read aloud item 1. Point out the word below the blank. Ask: *What short word can take the place of* **Omar**? (**he**) *Write* **He** *in the blank.* Then read the completed sentence aloud. Repeat for items 2–4.

Convention: Review the rule. Ask: *What word is* **can't** *short for?* (**cannot**) Then read aloud the sentence before having students complete the activity.

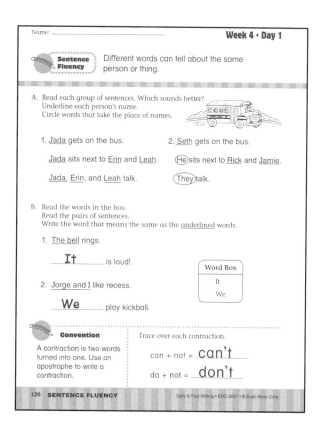

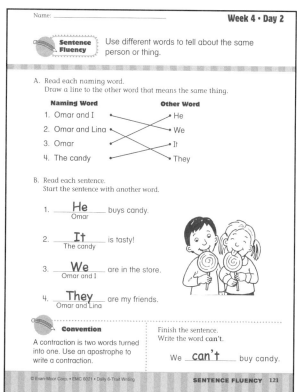

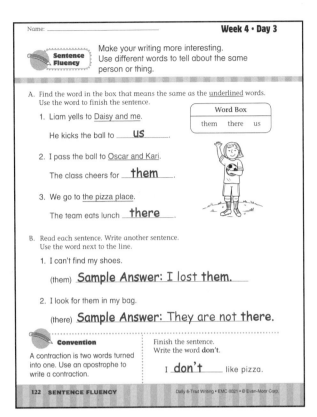

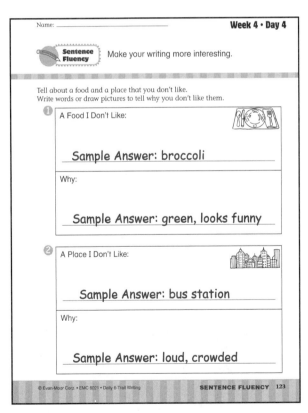

Name: _____ **Week 4 · Day 3**

Sentence Fluency

Make your writing more interesting. Use different words to tell about the same person or thing.

A. Find the word in the box that means the same as the <u>underlined</u> words. Use the word to finish the sentence.

Word Box
them   there   us

1. Liam yells to <u>Daisy and me</u>.

   He kicks the ball to ____ **us** ____.

2. I pass the ball to <u>Oscar and Kari</u>.

   The class cheers for ____ **them** ____.

3. We go to <u>the pizza place</u>.

   The team eats lunch ____ **there** ____.

B. Read each sentence. Write another sentence. Use the word next to the line.

1. I can't find my shoes.

   (them) **Sample Answer: I lost them.**

2. I look for them in my bag.

   (there) **Sample Answer: They are not there.**

Convention

A contraction is two words turned into one. Use an apostrophe to write a contraction.

Finish the sentence. Write the word **don't**.

I **don't** ____ like pizza.

122 SENTENCE FLUENCY   Daily 6-Trait Writing · EMC 6021 · © Evan-Moor Corp.

Name: _____ **Week 4 · Day 4**

Sentence Fluency

Make your writing more interesting.

Tell about a food and a place that you don't like. Write words or draw pictures to tell why you don't like them.

❶ A Food I Don't Like:

   Sample Answer: broccoli

   Why:

   Sample Answer: green, looks funny

❷ A Place I Don't Like:

   Sample Answer: bus station

   Why:

   Sample Answer: loud, crowded

© Evan-Moor Corp. · EMC 6021 · Daily 6-Trait Writing   **SENTENCE FLUENCY   123**

DAY 3

Review the rule. Say: *When we use different words to tell about the same things, we make our writing more interesting. Those different words help our sentences flow.* Then guide students through the activities. For example:

- **Activity A:** Read aloud the words in the box and have students repeat after you. Then read aloud item 1. Ask: *Which word can take the place of **Daisy and me**?* (**us**) Have students write the word on the line and read the completed sentence aloud. Repeat for items 2 and 3.

- **Activity B:** Read aloud item 1. Say: *Let's make up another sentence about the shoes that has the word **them** in it. When you can't find something, what does that mean?* (It is lost.) *We could say "I lost **them**."* Write the sentence on the board for students to copy. Repeat for item 2.

Convention: Read the rule and sentence aloud before students complete the activity.

DAY 4

Review the rule. Then guide students through the activity. For example:

- For item 1, ask: *What are some foods you don't like?* List students' answers on the board. Then have them choose one and copy it onto the first line.

- Ask: *Why don't you like that food?* List students' answers as phrases, such as "tastes icky" or "feels slimy." Have students choose a phrase and write it on the second line and draw a picture of the food. Repeat the process for item 2.

DAY 5 *Writing Prompt*

- Have students choose the food or place they wrote about on Day 4. Have them write a sentence beginning with *I don't like* ____. Then post the words *it*, **they**, and **there**. Have students write another sentence, using one of these words. For example: *I don't like the basement. It is dark and stinky down there.*

- Remind students to spell **don't** correctly.

Sentence Fluency Different words can tell about the same person or thing.

A. Read each group of sentences. Which sounds better?
Underline each person's name.
Circle words that take the place of names.

1. Jada gets on the bus.

   Jada sits next to Erin and Leah.

   Jada, Erin, and Leah talk.

2. Seth gets on the bus.

   He sits next to Rick and Jamie.

   They talk.

B. Read the words in the box.
Read the pairs of sentences.
Write the word that means the same as the <u>underlined</u> words.

1. <u>The bell</u> rings.

   _____ is loud!

2. <u>Jorge and I</u> like recess.

   _____ play kickball.

Word Box
It
We

Convention

A contraction is two words turned into one. Use an apostrophe to write a contraction.

Trace over each contraction.

can + not = <u>can't</u>

do + not = <u>don't</u>

 **Sentence Fluency**   Use different words to tell about the same person or thing.

A. Read each naming word.
Draw a line to the other word that means the same thing.

Naming Word   **Other Word**

1. Omar and I   •   • He

2. Omar and Lina •   • We

3. Omar   •   • It

4. The candy   •   • They

B. Read each sentence.
Start the sentence with another word.

1. _____ buys candy.
    Omar

2. _____ is tasty!
    The candy

3. _____ are in the store.
    Omar and I

4. _____ are my friends.
    Omar and Lina

 Convention

A contraction is two words turned into one. Use an apostrophe to write a contraction.

Finish the sentence.
Write the word **can't**.

We _____ buy candy.

Name: _____

 **Sentence Fluency**

Make your writing more interesting.
Use different words to tell about the same
person or thing.

A. Find the word in the box that means the same as the underlined words.
    Use the word to finish the sentence.

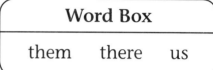

Word Box		
them	there	us

1. Liam yells to Daisy and me.

    He kicks the ball to _____.

2. I pass the ball to Oscar and Kari.

    The class cheers for _____.

3. We go to the pizza place.

    The team eats lunch _____.

B. Read each sentence. Write another sentence.
    Use the word next to the line.

1. I can't find my shoes.

    (them) _____

2. I look for them in my bag.

    (there) _____

 Convention

A contraction is two words turned
into one. Use an apostrophe to
write a contraction.

Finish the sentence.
Write the word **don't**.

I _____ like pizza.

Sentence Fluency

Make your writing more interesting.

Tell about a food and a place that you don't like.
Write words or draw pictures to tell why you don't like them.

1 A Food I Don't Like:

_____

Why:

_____

2 A Place I Don't Like:

_____

Why:

_____

DAY 1

Review the rule. Then guide students through the activities. For example:

- **Activity A:** Read the first sentence for item 1. Say: *We know who the sentence is about—Joel. We know that there is a boat.* Then ask: *Does the sentence tell us* **what** *Joel is doing in the boat?* (no) Then read the second sentence aloud. Ask: *What does Joel do in the boat?* (**sits**) Say: *That's what was missing from the first sentence. The first sentence is* not *a complete sentence. Let's cross out the first sentence.* Repeat the process for item 2.

- **Activity B:** Read aloud each word choice. Then point to the first word. (**cold**) Say: *I could write about something that is cold. Another word is* **water**. Ask: *Can I make the sentence "The water is cold"? Do I have all of the words?* (yes) Write the sentence on the board for students to copy. Repeat the process to create two more sentences.

Convention: Read the rule aloud. Say: *The contraction* **I'm** *is the words* **I** *and* **am** *put together.* Have students repeat the word **I'm** and complete the activity.

DAY 2

Review the rule. Then guide students through the activities. For example:

- Point out the word boxes. Say: *We'll use these naming, describing, and action words to write sentences about the picture.* Then have students repeat after you as you read aloud the words in each box.

- Point out the lizard. Ask: *Which animal is this?* (a lizard) Say: **Lizard** *starts with* **l**. *We can make a fun sentence with other words that start with* **l**. Ask: *Which describing and action words also start with* **l**? (**little, loud, laughs**) Ask: *How would the sentence sound with* **little**? (**The little lizard laughs.**) Have students trace over the words. Repeat the process for the bee, hippo, and tiger.

Convention: Review the rule. Then have students write the word on the line. Read aloud the completed sentence and have students repeat it.

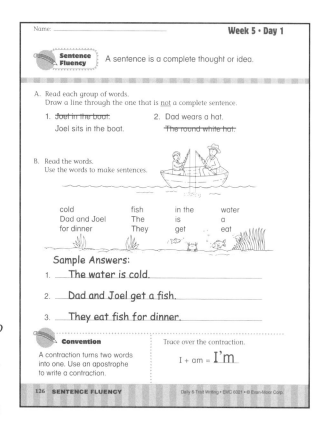

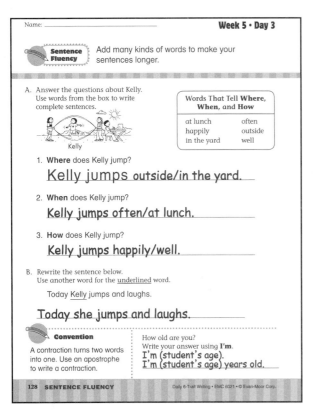

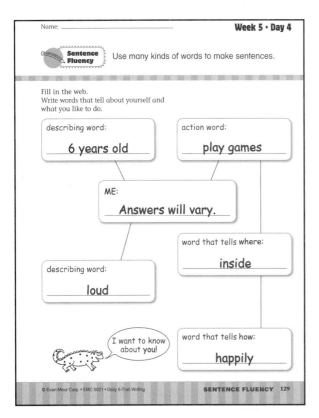

DAY 3

Review the rule. Then guide students through the activities. For example:

- **Activity A:** Read aloud the words and phrases in the box and have students repeat them. Then read aloud item 1. Ask: *Which word or words tell where Kelly jumps?* (**in the yard, outside**) Have students trace over the sentence starter and choose **in the yard** or **outside** to complete the sentence. Repeat the process for items 2 and 3.

- **Activity B:** Read the sentence aloud. Say: *We've written a lot of sentences with the word **Kelly** in them. What smaller word can take the place of **Kelly**?* (**she**) Have students rewrite the sentence, replacing **Kelly** with **she**.

Convention: Review the rule and read aloud the question. Model answering in a complete sentence, using "I'm (age)" or "I'm (age) years old." Then have students write their own sentences.

DAY 4

Review the rule. Then guide students through the activity. For example:

- Have students write their names in the center box. Then point out the boxes on the left. Ask: *What are some words or phrases that describe you?* (e.g., funny, smart, strong) List possible answers on the board. Then have students choose two and copy them in the boxes.

- Repeat the process for the boxes on the right, helping students brainstorm things they like to do and where and how the actions are done.

DAY 5 *Writing Prompt*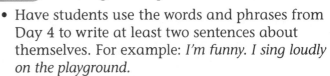

- Have students use the words and phrases from Day 4 to write at least two sentences about themselves. For example: *I'm funny. I sing loudly on the playground.*

- Remind students to spell **I'm** correctly.

Name: _____

 **Sentence Fluency**   A sentence is a complete thought or idea.

A. Read each group of words.
    Draw a line through the one that is <u>not</u> a complete sentence.

1. Joel in the boat.

    Joel sits in the boat.

2. Dad wears a hat.

    The round white hat.

B. Read the words.
    Use the words to make sentences.

cold	fish	in the	water
Dad and Joel	The	is	a
for dinner	They	get	eat

1. _____

2. _____

3. _____

 Convention

A contraction turns two words
into one. Use an apostrophe
to write a contraction.

Trace over the contraction.

I + am = $\underline{\text{I'm}}$

 **Sentence Fluency**   Write sentences that are fun to read aloud.

Look at the picture.
Read the words in the boxes.
Find words that begin with the same letter.
Use them to write sentences about the picture.

Naming Words	
bee	lizard
hippo	tiger

Describing Words	
big	little
hot	loud
huge	tired

Action Words
buzzes
hides
laughs
takes a nap

1. <u>The little lizard laughs.</u> _____

2. _____

3. _____

4. _____

 Convention

A contraction turns two words into one. Use an apostrophe to write a contraction.

Finish the sentence.
Write the word **I'm**.

_____ a super student!

Sentence Fluency Add many kinds of words to make your sentences longer.

A. Answer the questions about Kelly. Use words from the box to write complete sentences.

Kelly

Words That Tell **Where**, **When**, and **How**	
at lunch	often
happily	outside
in the yard	well

1. **Where** does Kelly jump?

Kelly jumps _____

2. **When** does Kelly jump?

_____

3. **How** does Kelly jump?

_____

B. Rewrite the sentence below.
Use another word for the <u>underlined</u> word.

Today Kelly jumps and laughs.

_____

Convention

A contraction turns two words into one. Use an apostrophe to write a contraction.

How old are you?
Write your answer using **I'm**.

_____

Sentence Fluency Use many kinds of words to make sentences.

Fill in the web.
Write words that tell about yourself and
what you like to do.

describing word:

_____

action word:

_____

ME:

_____

word that tells **where**:

_____

describing word:

_____

I want to know
about **you!**

word that tells **how**:

_____

VOICE
Tell How You Feel

Refer to pages 6 and 7 to introduce or review the writing trait.

DAY 1

Say: *You may know the word voice to mean the sound you make when you speak. This week, we will learn about a different kind of voice.* Then read the rule aloud and guide students through the activities. For example:

- **Activity A:** Write the word **voice** on the board. Say the word aloud and have students repeat it.

- **Activity B:** For item 1, say: *Bored is a feeling.* Ask: *What does it mean?* (You are not interested in what you are doing.) Have students trace over the word and say it aloud. Then have students repeat after you as you read each sentence with expression. Ask: *Which sentence sounds like the writer is bored?* (the fourth) Have students draw a line from the sentence to the word. Repeat the process for each word.

Convention: Read the rule aloud. Write the two words on the board and have students repeat them after you. Say: *We need to be careful when we spell these words. Today, we'll practice h-e-a-r. You hear with your ears.* Point out how the word **ear** is in **hear**. Read the sentence aloud as students fill it in.

DAY 2

Read the rule aloud. Then guide students through the activities. For example:

- **Activity A:** Read aloud the interjections in the box and have students repeat them. If necessary, explain the connotation of each one. Then point out the girl in the first picture. Say: *This girl is on a roller coaster.* Ask: *What is she feeling?* (happy, excited) *Which word would she say?* (**Whee!**) Have students write the word on the line. Repeat the process for items 2–4.

- **Activity B:** Assign partners. Then model sharing a memory, using a word in the word box. For example: *Ick! makes me think of the time I caught a fish. I had to hold it. It was slimy!* Then have students share their own memories for a word with their partners.

Convention: Review the rule. Say: *Here with two e's means where you are right now.* Read the sentence aloud before students fill it in.

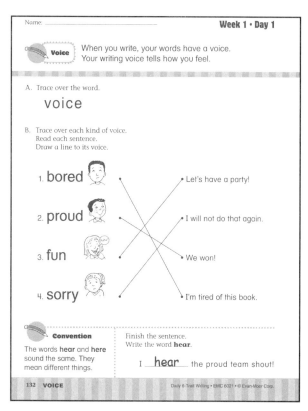

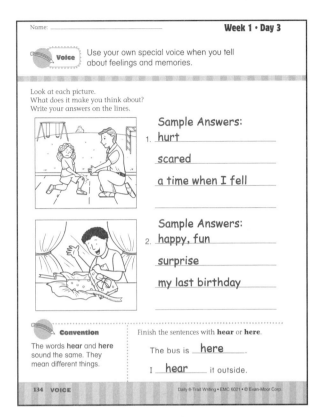

DAY 3

Read the rule aloud. Say: *Each of us has our own voice that we use when we write.* Then guide students through the activities. For example:

- Have students describe the first picture. (A girl is hurt.) Ask: *What feelings does it make you think of?* Write possibilities on the board. Model recalling a similar memory. For example, say: *Once, I fell off my bike and hurt myself, too. I had cuts all over my leg! I had to go to the nurse.* List words and phrases such as **Ouch!**, **fell**, and **go to the nurse**.

- Have students think of a similar memory and write words or phrases related to it. Explain that each student's memory will differ; there is no "right" answer. You may want to allow the use of creative spelling so students can express individual ideas. Repeat the process for the second picture. If time permits, compare students' work, highlighting the individuality of each one.

Convention: Review the two word meanings. Then read aloud each sentence before students fill it in.

DAY 4

Review the rule. Then guide students through the activities. For example:

- **Activity A:** Review the meaning of **proud**. (feeling good about something you've done) Help students brainstorm a time when they felt proud, such as learning to ride a bike. Circulate and offer support in choosing a personal experience to draw.

- **Activity B:** Ask: *What does a proud face look like?* (smiling) Encourage students to think of their own way to complete the face and speech bubble.

DAY 5 *Writing Prompt*

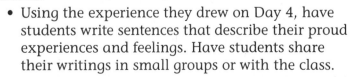

- Using the experience they drew on Day 4, have students write sentences that describe their proud experiences and feelings. Have students share their writings in small groups or with the class.

- Remind students to spell **hear** and **here** correctly.

Name: _____

 **Voice**   When you write, your words have a voice.
Your writing voice tells how you feel.

A. Trace over the word.

voice

B. Trace over each kind of voice.
Read each sentence.
Draw a line to its voice.

1. bored •   • Let's have a party!

2. proud •   • I will not do that again.

3. fun •   • We won!

4. sorry •   • I'm tired of this book.

 Convention

The words **hear** and **here** sound the same. They mean different things.

Finish the sentence.
Write the word **hear**.

I _____ the proud team shout!

 **Voice**   What you say tells how you feel.

A. Look at the pictures.
    What does each person say?
    Write a word from the box on the line.

Word Box
Ick!   Whee!   Yikes!   Yum!

B. Say each word in the word box to a partner.
    Tell about a time you used one word.

 Convention

The words **hear** and **here** sound the same. They mean different things.

Finish the sentence.
Write the word **here**.

My friend is _____.

 **Voice** Use your own special voice when you tell about feelings and memories.

Look at each picture.
What does it make you think about?
Write your answers on the lines.

1. _____

_____

_____

_____

2. _____

_____

_____

_____

 Convention

The words **hear** and **here** sound the same. They mean different things.

Finish the sentences with **hear** or **here**.

The bus is _____.

I _____ it outside.

 **Voice**   Use your own special voice when you tell about feelings and memories.

A. Think of a time when you felt proud.
   Draw a picture of what happened.

B. Finish the face.
   Show what you looked like when you felt proud.
   Write what you said.

DAY 1

Read the rule aloud and review the meaning of **voice**. (how a writer feels about a topic) Then guide students through the activities. For example:

- **Activity A:** For item 1, say: *We can write in a cheerful voice. What does that mean?* (Our writing sounds happy.) Have students trace over the word and say it aloud. Then read the sentences aloud in a cheerful tone. Ask: *Why is the writer cheerful?* (She wants school to start; she thinks she will have fun.) Say: *The words **can't wait** and **fun** give clues that the writer is cheerful. They give the writing a cheerful voice. Let's circle those words.* Repeat for items 2–4.

- **Activity B:** Read item 1. Then model determining whether each word fits with a grumpy voice. Say: *Grumpy people would probably say they **don't like** something. They might be **angry**, too. But would they say **yay**?* (no) Have students circle the word. Repeat the process for item 2.

DAY 2

Read the rule aloud. Say: *Your voice is all about you! Use it to tell about yourself.* Then guide students through the activities. For example:

- **Activity A:** Say: *This is a letter from Max to his new friend Cindy. Max tells her about himself.* Then read the letter aloud. Ask: *What is Max like?* (e.g., He has brown hair. He has a sister, Kara.) Say: *You can tell many different things about yourself. Let's underline everything that tells about Max.*

  Convention: Point out the letter's greeting. Say: *When you write a letter, you start it with a greeting, such as **Dear**.* Then point out the closing. Say: *You end a letter with a closing, such as **Your new friend,** and write your name. Begin both the greeting and the closing with capital letters.*

- **Activity B:** Read item 1. Invite students to tell how they help at home. Write a few answers on the board. Then have students write their own answers. Repeat the process for items 2 and 3. Then have students draw a self-portrait in the space provided. If time permits, compare students' responses, highlighting their individuality.

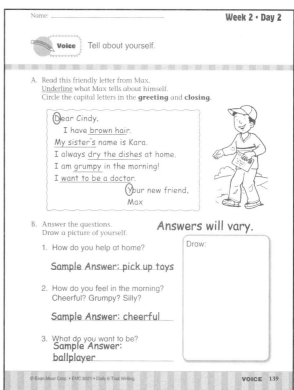

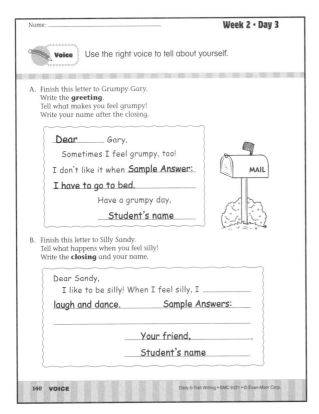

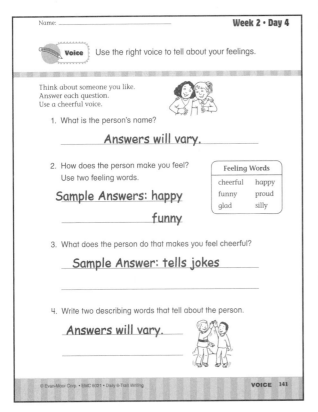

DAY 3

DAY 3

Read the rule aloud. Then guide students through the activities. For example:

- **Activity A:** Review what a greeting is in a letter. Write **Dear** on the board and have students copy it onto the line. Then say: *We are writing to Grumpy Gary. This letter should have a grumpy voice!* Read the first two sentences aloud. Ask: *When do you feel grumpy? In the morning? When you're hungry?* Invite students to share responses before writing them. Then have students write their names after the closing.

- **Activity B:** As with Activity A, prompt students to fill in the sentences with their own answers. Suggest a closing, such as **Your friend**. Write the phrase and have students copy it.

Convention: Point out how each greeting and closing begins with a capital letter.

DAY 4

Read the rule aloud. Then guide students through the activity. For example:

- Say: *We will write letters to someone we like.* Then read question 1. Help students brainstorm someone they like, such as a friend or family member. Have them write the name of that person.

- For questions 2 and 3, have students brainstorm with a partner before writing. Circulate and help them formulate responses. For item 4, encourage the use of words that describe personality traits, such as **friendly**, rather than physical attributes, such as **tall**.

DAY 5 *Writing Prompt*

- Have students write a letter to the person they chose for Day 4, including a greeting, closing, and two or three sentences written in a cheerful voice. If necessary, model writing a letter on the board.

- Remind students to capitalize the greeting and closing of the letter.

 **Voice**   Use words that match your voice.

A. Trace over each kind of voice.
   Read the sentences next to it.
   Circle the word or words that show the voice.

1. cheerful    I can't wait for school to start!
   I will do many fun things.

2. grumpy    Peas are icky.
   I don't want to eat my dinner.

3. silly    I put on my funny wig and nose.
   I pretend I'm a clown!

4. serious    Be safe when you cross the street.
   Look out for cars.

B. Read the words.
   Circle the word or words that do <u>not</u> belong with each voice.

1. **grumpy:**   don't like   angry   yay

2. **serious:**   help me   yummy   careful

Voice   Tell about yourself.

A. Read this friendly letter from Max.
    <u>Underline</u> what Max tells about himself.
    Circle the capital letters in the **greeting** and **closing**.

> Ⓓear Cindy,
>   I have brown hair.
> My sister's name is Kara.
> I always dry the dishes at home.
> I am grumpy in the morning!
> I want to be a doctor.
>   Your new friend,
>   Max

B. Answer the questions.
    Draw a picture of yourself.

1. How do you help at home?

    _____

2. How do you feel in the morning?
    Cheerful? Grumpy? Silly?

    _____

3. What do you want to be?

    _____

Draw:

 **Voice**   Use the right voice to tell about yourself.

A. Finish this letter to Grumpy Gary.
    Write the **greeting**.
    Tell what makes you feel grumpy!
    Write your name after the closing.

> _____ Gary,
>
>   Sometimes I feel grumpy, too!
>
> I don't like it when _____
>
> _____
>
>   Have a grumpy day,
>
>   _____

MAIL

B. Finish this letter to Silly Sandy.
    Tell what happens when you feel silly!
    Write the **closing** and your name.

> Dear Sandy,
>   I like to be silly! When I feel silly, I _____
>
> _____
>
> _____
>
>   _____ ,
>
> _____

 **Voice**   Use the right voice to tell about your feelings.

Think about someone you like.
Answer each question.
Use a cheerful voice.

1. What is the person's name?

    _____

2. How does the person make you feel?
    Use two feeling words.

    _____

    _____

Feeling Words	
cheerful	happy
funny	proud
glad	silly

3. What does the person do that makes you feel cheerful?

    _____

    _____

4. Write two describing words that tell about the person.

    _____

    _____

DAY 1

Ask: *Have you ever seen a movie that made you scared? Have you ever read a story that made you laugh?* Then read the rule aloud. Say: *A movie, a story, or any kind of writing has a mood. Today, we'll learn different kinds of moods.* Then guide students through the activities. For example:

- For item 1, say: *If a story makes you a little scared and you wonder what's going to happen, it has a spooky mood.* Have students trace over the word. Repeat the process for each word, defining it if necessary.

- Return to item 1 and say: *Let's find the picture and words that have a spooky mood.* Point out the first pair of sentences on the right and read them. Ask: *Does the dog look spooky? Is something spooky happening?* (no) Continue to go through each pair until students identify the "spooky" one. (the last) Have students draw a line to it. Repeat the process for items 2–5.

Convention: Review the rule. Then read aloud the sentence before students complete the activity.

DAY 2

Read the rule aloud. Then guide students through the activities. For example:

- Point to item 1. Say: *Let's find the words that are spooky.* Read the first word. Ask: *Is a ghost spooky?* (yes) Say: *Ghost is a good word to use if you want to create a spooky mood. Let's circle it.* Repeat the process for each word, explaining that a clown is <u>not</u> spooky, so it doesn't fit a spooky mood.

- Then ask: *What are some other spooky words? What kinds of things do you find in spooky stories?* (e.g., shadow, cobweb, dark) Write the words on the board. Say: *We can use all of these words to write in a spooky voice and to create a spooky mood.* Have students choose words to copy onto their papers or think of their own "spooky" words to write. Repeat the process for each item.

Convention: Review the rule. Then read aloud the question before students complete the activity.

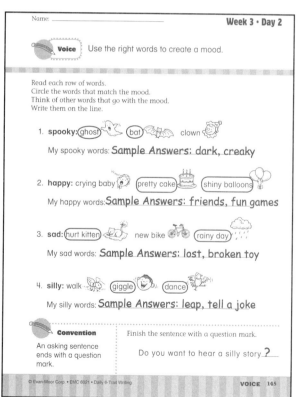

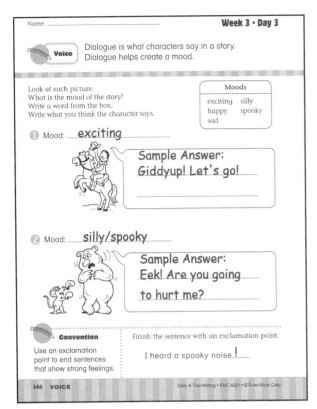

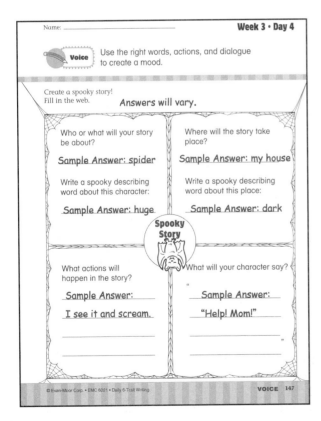

DAY 3

Read the rule aloud. Then say: *Characters are the people or animals in a story. They can say something spooky, silly, happy, sad, or exciting.* Then guide students through the activities. For example:

- For item 1, ask: *What is happening in this picture?* (A cowboy is on his horse.) *Which kind of mood does this show?* (exciting) Have students write the word on the line.

- Encourage students to think of a storyline to go with the picture. (e.g., The cowboy must round up his cattle.) Then ask: *What do you think a cowboy would say in this story?* Remind students that it should sound exciting. Write students' ideas for dialogue on the board. Have students copy the words or write their own ideas. Repeat the process for item 2.

Convention: Review the rule. Read aloud the activity and say: *If I heard a spooky noise, I would be very afraid! This writer shows a strong emotion, so we end this sentence with an exclamation point.*

DAY 4

Read the rule aloud. Then guide students through the activity. For example:

- Say: *Let's create a spooky story together!* Then read aloud the question in the first box. Ask: *Who would be in a spooky story?* As a class, decide on a character. Write the word on the board for students to copy onto their papers.

- Continue to answer the questions as a class, reminding students that the mood of the story is spooky. Encourage them to choose story elements and describing words accordingly.

DAY 5 *Writing Prompt*

- Have students write two or three sentences to tell a spooky story. Students should use words, actions, and dialogue from Day 4.

- Encourage students to use question marks and exclamation points to convey the mood of the story.

 **Voice** All writing has a mood.
A mood is how the writing makes you feel.

Trace over each mood.
Look at each picture and read the sentences.
Draw a line from the mood to its sentences.

1. __spooky__ •

• Rex is lost.
  He howls for Leo.

2. __sad__ •

• Oh, what a surprise!
  Cow and Pig exercise.

3. __silly__ •

• Off we go!
  Let's find a new land!

4. __exciting__ •

• I hug Grandma.
  I love her.

5. __happy__ •

• The house is scary.
  Who lives there?

 Convention

A telling sentence
ends with a period.

Finish the sentence with a period.

It was a sad movie____

 **Voice**   Use the right words to create a mood.

Read each row of words.
Circle the words that match the mood.
Think of other words that go with the mood.
Write them on the line.

1. **spooky:** ghost   bat   clown

   My spooky words: _____

2. **happy:** crying baby   pretty cake   shiny balloons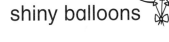

   My happy words: _____

3. **sad:** hurt kitten   new bike   rainy day

   My sad words: _____

4. **silly:** walk   giggle   dance

   My silly words: _____

 Convention

An asking sentence
ends with a question
mark.

Finish the sentence with a question mark.

Do you want to hear a silly story_____

 **Voice**   Dialogue is what characters say in a story.
Dialogue helps create a mood.

Look at each picture.
What is the mood of the story?
Write a word from the box.
Write what you think the character says.

Moods	
exciting	silly
happy	spooky
sad	

① Mood: _____

② Mood: _____

 Convention

Use an exclamation
point to end sentences
that show strong feelings.

Finish the sentence with an exclamation point.

I heard a spooky noise_____

 **Voice** Use the right words, actions, and dialogue to create a mood.

Create a spooky story!
Fill in the web.

Who or what will your story be about?

_____

Write a spooky describing word about this character:

_____

Where will the story take place?

_____

Write a spooky describing word about this place:

_____

Spooky Story

What actions will happen in the story?

_____

_____

_____

_____

What will your character say?

"_____

_____

_____

_____"

DAY 1

Read the rule aloud. Then say: *This week, we will learn about rhyming words and poems. A poem is a special kind of writing that can use rhyming words. People who write poems use strong voice.* Guide students through the activities. For example:

- **Activity A:** Say: *Listen for the words that rhyme.* Then read aloud the words in item 1 and have students repeat them. Ask: *Which words rhyme?* (**frog** and **log**) Have students circle the words. Then ask: *What is another word that has the same ending sound as frog and log?* If necessary, write **og** on the board and ask: *What word do I get if I put a d in front of og?* (**dog**) Repeat for items 2–4.

- **Activity B:** Say: *Listen for the words that rhyme in this poem.* Read aloud the first poem and have students repeat each line after you. Ask: *Which words have the same ending sounds?* (**fox** and **rocks**) Have students circle the words. Point out that rhyming words don't always end with the same letters, even though they sound the same. Repeat the process for "My Note."

Convention: Read the rule aloud. Then point out the poem titles in Activity B. Have students circle the capital letters. Then have students complete the activity for *Roses Are Red*.

DAY 2

Read the rule aloud. Then guide students through the activities. For example:

- Read aloud the words in the box. Have students repeat them after you.

- Read aloud poem 1. Say: *We need a word that rhymes with set. Look at the words in the box. Which words rhyme with set?* (**let** and **wet**) Read the second line of the poem with **let** and then **wet**. Ask: *Which word makes sense with the poem?* (**wet**) Have students write the word on the line and read aloud the completed poem. Repeat the process for items 2–4.

Convention: Read the rule aloud. Then point out how each line in items 1–4 starts with a capital letter. Read aloud the poem in the activity before students trace over the capital letters.

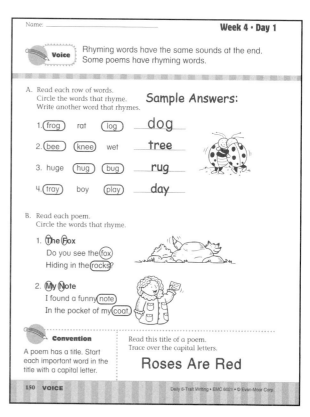

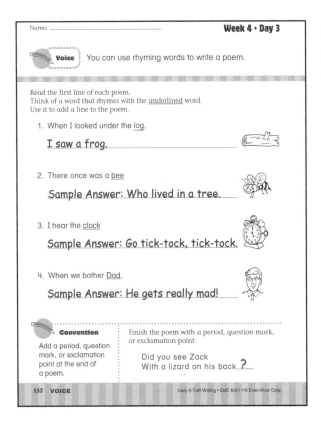

Name: _____   **Week 4 • Day 3**

✎ **Voice** You can use rhyming words to write a poem.

Read the first line of each poem.
Think of a word that rhymes with the underlined word.
Use it to add a line to the poem.

1. When I looked under the log,

   I saw a frog.

2. There once was a bee

   Sample Answer: Who lived in a tree.

3. I hear the clock

   Sample Answer: Go tick-tock, tick-tock.

4. When we bother Dad,

   Sample Answer: He gets really mad!

✎ **Convention**

Add a period, question
mark, or exclamation
point at the end of
a poem.

Finish the poem with a period, question mark,
or exclamation point.

Did you see Zack
With a lizard on his back **?**

152 VOICE   Daily 6-Trait Writing • EMC 6021 • © Evan-Moor Corp.

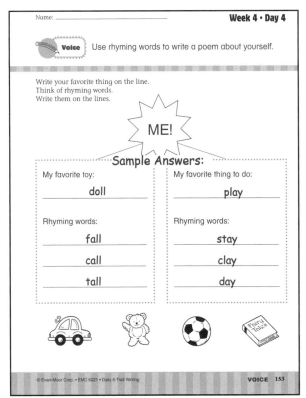

Name: _____   **Week 4 • Day 4**

✎ **Voice** Use rhyming words to write a poem about yourself.

Write your favorite thing on the line.
Think of rhyming words.
Write them on the lines.

ME!

Sample Answers:

My favorite toy: doll

Rhyming words:
fall
call
tall

My favorite thing to do: play

Rhyming words:
stay
clay
day

© Evan-Moor Corp. • EMC 6021 • Daily 6-Trait Writing   **VOICE 153**

DAY 3

Review the rule. Then guide students through the activities. For example:

- Say: *We're going to make up rhyming poems. The first line of each poem is written for us. We'll write the second line.* Read aloud item 1. Ask: *What rhymes with log?* Write answers on the board.

- Model using a word to finish the poem. For example, say: ***Frog** rhymes with **log**. You might see a frog under a log. So, we could write "When I looked under the log,/I saw a frog."* Write the line on the board and have students copy it onto their papers. Repeat the process for items 2–4, encouraging students to think of their own ideas. Assist students in writing down their ideas.

Convention: Read the rule aloud. After reading the poem, say: *This poem is asking something. What kind of mark do we use when we ask?* (question mark) Have students write it on the line.

DAY 4

Review the rule. Then say: *You can use poems to tell what makes you special. Today, we'll think of rhyming words that tell about us!* Then guide students through the activity. For example:

- Direct students' attention to the first box. Have them write their favorite toy on the line.

- Model finding a rhyming word. For example, say: *A car is my favorite toy.* Ask: *What words rhyme with **car**?* Prompt students to replace the **c** with other letters to find words such as **far** or **star**. Have them do the same with their own answers. Repeat for the second box. Or, students may complete the first task in each box, and then brainstorm with a partner to find rhyming words.

DAY 5 *Writing Prompt* ✎

- Have students use their rhyming words from Day 4 to write two two-line poems about themselves. Remind students that the rhyming words belong at the end of each line.

- Direct students to use correct capitalization and punctuation in the title and poem.

 **Voice**   Rhyming words have the same sounds at the end.
Some poems have rhyming words.

A. Read each row of words.
Circle the words that rhyme.
Write another word that rhymes.

1. frog   rat   log   ___dog___

2. bee   knee   wet   _____

3. huge   hug   bug   _____

4. tray   boy   play   _____

B. Read each poem.
Circle the words that rhyme.

1. **The Fox**

   Do you see the fox
   Hiding in the rocks?

2. **My Note**

   I found a funny note
   In the pocket of my coat.

 Convention

A poem has a title. Start each important word in the title with a capital letter.

Read this title of a poem.
Trace over the capital letters.

Roses Are Red

 **Voice** Some poems use rhyming words.

Read each poem.
Find the words in the box that
rhyme with the underlined word.
Write the best word on the line.

Word Box			
take	clock	let	map
cake	sock	wet	nap

1. Get ready, get <u>set</u>.

   It's time to get _____!

2. Jack uses his <u>cap</u>

   To take his morning _____.

3. The birds in the <u>flock</u>

   Sit on top of the _____.

4. Look out for the <u>snake</u>.

   He's hiding in the _____!

 Convention

You can start each
line of a poem with
a capital letter.

Trace over the capital letters in this poem.

There's a big black bug
Swimming in my mug!

 **Voice** You can use rhyming words to write a poem.

Read the first line of each poem.
Think of a word that rhymes with the <u>underlined</u> word.
Use it to add a line to the poem.

1. When I looked under the <u>log</u>,

   _____

2. There once was a <u>bee</u>

   _____

3. I hear the <u>clock</u>

   _____

4. When we bother <u>Dad</u>,

   _____

 **Convention**

Add a period, question mark, or exclamation point at the end of a poem.

Finish the poem with a period, question mark, or exclamation point.

   Did you see Zack
   With a lizard on his back_____

 **Voice**   Use rhyming words to write a poem about yourself.

Write your favorite thing on the line.
Think of rhyming words.
Write them on the lines.

ME!

My favorite toy:	My favorite thing to do:
_____	_____
Rhyming words:	Rhyming words:
_____	_____
_____	_____
_____	_____

DAY 1

Read the rule aloud. Then guide students through the activities. For example:

- **Activity A:** Read aloud the first sentence starter. Then invite students to tell how they feel when school begins each day. Emphasize that each student may feel differently; there is no "right" answer. Repeat these steps for sentences 2 and 3. You may want to allow use of creative spelling in order for students to express individual thoughts.

- **Activity B:** Have each student choose a sentence from Activity A and draw a picture to describe the situation and feeling. Encourage students to use facial features and expressions to portray their feelings. (e.g., a smile, closed eyes)

Convention: Read the rule aloud. Model writing today's date. Then have students complete the activity.

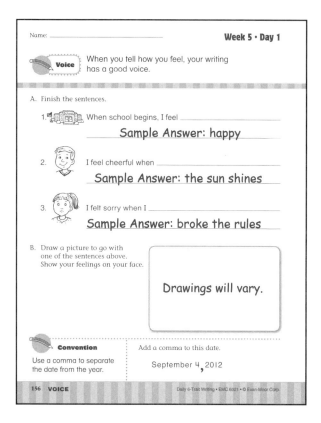

DAY 2

Read the rule aloud. Then guide students through the activities. For example:

- **Activity A:** For the first line, ask: *Who is someone you love? Who would you like to write a poem about?* Guide students to write the name on the line. Then ask: *What are some words that describe that person?* Encourage students to go beyond physical descriptions. Write words on the board for them to copy, or allow creative spelling. Then have students work in pairs or small groups to brainstorm words that rhyme with the describing words. Guide students toward words with easy rhymes.

- **Activity B:** Model forming a poem. For example, say: *I'll write a poem called "My Dad." He is nice and kind. I'll use **nice** as my describing word. **Nice** rhymes with **twice**. I can write "My dad is so nice/I'll hug him twice."* Write the poem and point out how the rhyming words are at the end of each line. Remind students to give their poems a title.

Convention: Read the rule aloud. Display a letter or an example of one in a writing handbook. Review where the greeting is located. (at the beginning) Then have students complete the activity.

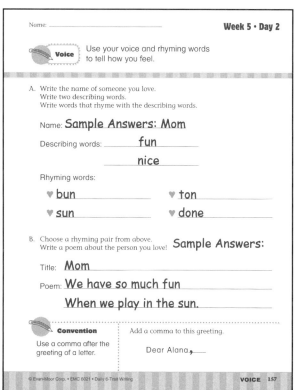

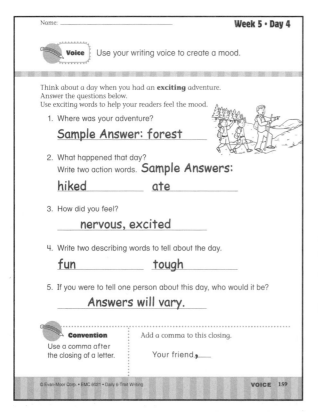

Read the rule aloud. Then guide students through the activity. For example:

- Read aloud each word in the word box and have students repeat them. Then point out the picture of the girl and the letter. Say: *Kristin is telling about what happened one day. From the look on her face, what kind of day do you think it was—happy or spooky?* (spooky) Say: *We'll help Kristin tell about her day by adding words that match a spooky mood.*

- Read the letter aloud. Then return to the first sentence. Ask: *Which word in the word box best describes Halloween?* Remind students that they need to choose a describing word. (**spooky**) Have students write the word on the line. Then guide students in completing the remaining sentences, as well as the second letter.

Read the rule aloud. Then guide students through the activities. For example:

- As a class, brainstorm times that were exciting, such as when the students did something unexpected or new. Then choose a time to write about.

- Have students write the answer to question 1. Then read aloud question 2. Invite students to think of powerful action words. Write possibilities on the board and have students choose two to copy onto their papers. Continue to guide students through the questions. For items 3–5, encourage students to come up with their own answers.

Convention: Read the rule aloud. Review where the closing of a letter is located and have students complete the activity.

- Have students write a friendly letter about the adventurous day they described on Day 4. Have students write at least three sentences, using their answers from items 1–4. Students should write the letter to the person they named in item 5.

- Remind students to use commas in the date, greeting, and closing of the letter.

 **Voice** When you tell how you feel, your writing has a good voice.

A. Finish the sentences.

1.  When school begins, I feel _____

_____

2. I feel cheerful when _____

_____

3.  I felt sorry when I _____

_____

B. Draw a picture to go with one of the sentences above. Show your feelings on your face.

 Convention

Use a comma to separate the date from the year.

Add a comma to this date.

September 4 2012

 **Voice** Use your voice and rhyming words to tell how you feel.

A. Write the name of someone you love.
    Write two describing words.
    Write words that rhyme with the describing words.

Name: _____

Describing words: _____

_____

Rhyming words:

♥ _____   ♥ _____

♥ _____   ♥ _____

B. Choose a rhyming pair from above.
    Write a poem about the person you love!

Title: _____

Poem: _____

_____

 Convention

Use a comma after the greeting of a letter.

Add a comma to this greeting.

Dear Alana_____

Voice

Use the right words to create a mood.

Read each letter.
Choose the best words in the box
to tell about the mood.
Write the words on the lines.

Word Box		
balloons	happy	spooky
ghosts	played	yelled

Dear Al,

    I had a very _____ Halloween.

Mom and Dad dressed up as _____.

I _____ when I saw them!

        Your cousin,

        Kristin

Dear Kristin,

    My birthday was a _____ day.

There were red and blue _____!

We _____ games all day.

        Love,

        Al

 **Voice**   Use your writing voice to create a mood.

Think about a day when you had an **exciting** adventure.
Answer the questions below.
Use exciting words to help your readers feel the mood.

1. Where was your adventure?

    _____

2. What happened that day?
   Write two action words.

    _____   _____

3. How did you feel?

    _____

4. Write two describing words to tell about the day.

    _____   _____

5. If you were to tell one person about this day, who would it be?

    _____

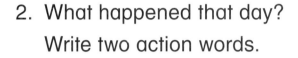 **Convention**
Use a comma after
the closing of a letter.

Add a comma to this closing.

Your friend_____

Proofreading Marks

Mark	Meaning	Example
℘	Take this out (delete).	I love ℘ to read.
⊙	Add a period.	It was late⊙
≡	Make this a capital letter.	First prize went to maria. ≡
/	Make this a lowercase letter.	We saw a /Black /Cat.
____	Fix the spelling.	This is our ~~hause~~. house
⋏	Add a comma.	Goodnight⋏Mom.
⌄	Add an apostrophe.	That⌄s Lil⌄s bike.
! ? ∧ ∧	Add an exclamation point or a question mark.	Help∧Can you help me∧ ! ?
∧	Add a word or a letter.	red The∧pen is mine.
# ∧	Add a space between words.	I like#pizza. ∧
____	Underline the words.	We read <u>Old Yeller</u>.

   Daily 6-Trait Writing • EMC 6021 • © Evan-Moor Corp.